The World in Your Cup

A handbook in the ancient art of tea leaf reading

Joseph F. Conroy

Emilie J. Conroy

DNA Press™

For information contact editors@dnapress.com.

Printed in the United States of America on acid-free paper
DNA Press website address: www.dnapress.com

First Edition 2006.

Library of Congress Cataloging-in-Publication Data

Conroy, Joseph F.
  The world in your cup : a handbook in the ancient art of tea leaf reading
/ Joseph F. Conroy, Emilie J. Conroy. — 1st ed.
       p. cm.

ISBN 1-933255-11-0

1. Fortune-telling by tea leaves. I. Conroy, Emilie J. II. Title.
  BF1881.C66 2006
  133.3'244—dc22

     2 0 0 6 0 1 1 3 3 5

DNA Press, LLC
P.O. BOX 572
Eagleville, PA 19408, USA
www.dnapress.com
editors@dnapress.com

Publisher: DNA Press, LLC
Executive Editor: Alexander Kuklin
Art Direction: Alex Nartea
Layout Design: Studio N Vision (www.studionvision.com)

About The Authors

We are a father-daughter writing team with backgrounds in World Languages, Psychology, Medieval History and Spirituality. With this book, we are engaged in our fourth collaboration. Our different experiences and academic backgrounds complement each other, and each of us brings a similar common sense approach to even the most unusual topics.

You may wonder how two nice people like us came to be interested in tasseomancy. We come from a long line of tea drinkers, so we have a familiarity with all kinds of teas. We also come from a family where various aunts, mothers and grandmothers would regularly offer to read tea leaves after dinners or in the afternoon. These readings were usually done for amusement, and neither one of us remembers any earth-shattering, life-changing pronouncements during one of these sessions.

Our main goals in creating this book were to provide you, the reader, with background information on tea, practical knowledge about tea leaf reading and a clear guide to doing readings on your own. With a bit of practice, you will soon amaze your friends and family with your command of this popular method of divination.

One note before we begin: we talked with a good number of people who do readings, and while they were willing to share their experiences and knowledge with us and you, they did not, for the most part, want their names or locations used in the book. For that reason, although we have accurately transmitted their words in this work, we have changed names and locales to preserve their privacy.

Dedication

In writing this book, we remember Anna and Grace, two of our strong ancestors; and we express our gratitude to Janet and Catherine Grace (wife/mother and daughter/sister), two of our strong contemporaries; and all those tea drinkers and leaf readers who contributed to our knowledge. Thank you!

Contents

Be sure to visit our website: **www.worldinyourcup.com**

Opening The Tea Tin

An introduction to the book.

"Please, ladies, take your seats," Mrs. Whittington says in her melodic voice.

The six ladies, all wearing their finest Victorian afternoon gowns, sit at a round table in the parlor. A servant wheels in the silver tea service on a cherrywood cart. She leaves the cart to Mrs. Whittington's right. Fine bone china cups with matching saucers in a fancy flower motif sit at each place. The hostess waits until the servant has left the parlor. She closes the sliding doors before speaking.

"Who will go first?" Mrs. Whittington asks with a warm smile. What she is about to do might have branded her a sorceress a few centuries ago.

"I shall," Mrs. Saint-James, a small woman almost lost under her fashionable finery, eagerly volunteers.

"Very well, Mrs. Saint-James, I shall pour."

With that, Mrs. Whittington takes an embossed metal canister, and spoons just the right amount of pure black tea into Mrs. Saint-James' cup. She pours the hot water and sits back.

Mrs. Saint-James, using a silver spoon, stirs the tea as it steeps. The other ladies watch with fascination. A feeling of the forbidden surrounds the whole activity. While tea leaf reading is quite common and not officially condemned, the practice retains a slightly naughty feeling.

Mrs. Saint-James puts down the spoon, picks up the delicate cup and drinks her tea. But not all of it. She leaves enough liquid in the bottom of the cup to cover the leaves, being careful not to disturb them.

"Excellent, my dear," says Mrs. Whittington as she takes Mrs. Saint-James' saucer and hands it to her. "Now, in one quick motion, please, place the saucer on top of the cup upside down, and turn the cup over."

Mrs. Saint-James does as instructed and places the saucer in the center of the table with the upside down cup on top. With a practiced movement, Mrs. Whittington turns the cup rightside up. Mrs. Saint-James and the other ladies look carefully into the cup.

"Now we shall begin our reading, Mrs. Saint-James," says Mrs. Whittington.

* * *

This may be what you picture when you hear the words "tea leaf reading," a quaint Victorian parlor with proper ladies indulging in a slightly questionable, but popular pastime. But the practice of looking into the future—and understanding the present—goes back a lot further than Victorian England.

When we think of tea, many images come to mind: mysterious Cathay, the vast network of traders and merchants, a refreshing hot or iced beverage, a wide variety of styles and flavors. We may also think of looking at the leaves at the bottom of a cup of tea and wondering if their shapes might have meaning, if their distribution around the cup might be able to tell us something of what is yet to come.

For millennia, people in many different lands and cultures have used tea leaves as a means of divination. "Having your tea leaves read" was a common occurrence in many places, and an activity that is still with us, gaining in popularity once again.

Tea leaf readings are certainly often associated with England, and remain popular there. The English believe that the practice was introduced into their land by the Romany—often inaccurately called Gypsies.

This is the other picture we might have in our minds: the prominent-featured woman with golden hoop earrings and a brightly-colored scarf covering her hair leaning forward over a cup of leaves and reading the fortune of her client.

When we learn that the Romany are the descendants of wanderers who trace their beginnings back to India, we come to have a better appreciation for the age of the practice of tea leaf reading. And we realize that, perhaps through the wanderings of the Romany, tea leaf reading has spread throughout Europe.

Once we reach India, it is not hard to imagine the practice stretching over the mountains and deserts into China. Both India and China claim to be the original tea-drinking lands. We know that the use of tea in China stretches back over five thousand years to its legendary discovery by an ancient emperor.

Other cultures developed leaf reading independently. The Sumerians apparently favored a kind of divination based on the remains of herbal teas in shallow clay cups. The Maya and Quechua peoples tell of seeing the future in mostly-drained bowls of maté or chocolate.

* * *

There is also a third image we have of tea leaf readings. It is the end of a family dinner. The plates have been cleared, the tea set brought in. The children and some of the adults have left the table. Those who remain know that this is a special time, a time of dimmed lights and hushed speech.

The tasseomancer of the evening, Grandmother Anna, Great Grandmother Grace, or one of the other experienced family members, begins by spooning leaves into each cup. Then hot water is poured and the tea steeps. After perhaps five minutes, the participants drink their tea, adding sugar according to taste, but never milk. The ladies in our family felt that milk, in clouding the tea, obscured the message of the leaves. The participants are careful to leave some liquid in the cup when they have finished.

Now comes the special moment. One person puts the saucer on top of the cup, and turns both pieces upside down, spilling most of the leaves onto the saucer. The cup is quickly turned rightside up again and placed on the saucer. The reader looks into the cup and begins to speak. The leaves yield their information, opening a small path into the future.

Tea leaf reading belongs in the wide field of divination. Over the millennia, human beings have tried to foretell the future by using all sorts of items as tokens. Candle wax dropped in water, the pattern of birds flying above, coins and sticks thrown on a table, all of these, and many more, have been used for divination. Such methods as the I Ching, the tarot and numerology belong in this field as well.

There are two formal names for tea leaf reading, *tasseomancy* and *tasseography*. The *tasse* part of the two words comes into English from French, where it means "cup." Reaching farther back, we find that *tasse* comes from Arabic, which borrowed the word from the Persian *tasht*, which means "tub, basin."

The ending of the first term, -*mancy*, has come from the French as well (-*mancie*), which in turn comes from the Late Latin *mantia*. Latin borrowed this term from the Greek *manteia* ("divination"), and the Greek word is from the noun *mantis*, "prophet." Thus *taaseomancy* is literally "cup divination."

The ending -*graphy* comes from the familiar Greek root *graph-*, "writing." *Tasseography* refers to divination based on the "writing," the layout, of the leaves in the cup. Both terms are used interchangeably today, and a quick check of the Internet for either word will reveal many sites. In this book, we have preferred to use *tasseomancy* and *tasseomancer*.

As in all forms of divination, the person doing the reading is the important factor in the activity. The tasseomancer must be able to enter the proper state of mind, clearing away all misleading thoughts, before attempting to interpret the tea leaves in the cup.

There are two major approaches to doing a tea leaf reading. The first method is based on the distribution of the leaves in the cup. Where the leaves are, how they are arranged and the patterns they make form the basis of the reader's statements. The second method is a bit more esoteric. The reader uses the leaves as a kind of Rorschach blot, soaking up information by being receptive to the other person's emanations, and using that information to help interpret the shapes in the cup.

In both methods, the reader will be able to make predictions about the future and statements to illuminate the present. Tea leaf reading is not used to find out about the past.

In this book we take a reasoned approach to the art of tea leaf reading, with the goal of enabling the reader to do accurate readings. We have divided the book into two large parts. In the first part, we present the history of tea and tasseomancy. We then move on to brewing tea and a special chapter on growing your own tea plants for tasseomancy. Once we have talked about tea, we look at the equipment—kettles, teapots, cups, saucers, infusion balls—needed to do a tea leaf reading.

The second part of the book deals with tasseomancy itself: how to prepare for the actual tea leaf reading. Here we discuss the importance of getting into the right frame of mind, and of setting the stage for the reading. We then discuss the shapes and positions the leaves may take in the cup and possible interpretations. We also give examples taken from actual readings. You will be able to look in the cup, see the leaves, and hear what interpretation an experienced tasseomancer gave.

Finally, because so many people have asked about this, we include a section on reading coffee grounds, and even the residue from hot chocolate. Once you have read through our guide to reading tea leaves in a cup, you will be able to apply this knowledge to reading all sorts of leaves and grounds, even herbal teas.

So, welcome to the amazing world of tasseomancy! We wish you success in your efforts, and hope that the leaves in your cup always foretell the most pleasant events.

Part One

Tea

Chapter One

A Brief History
Of Tea

The year is 2737 BCE. Thick mists cling to rolling green hills. Here in China, better known to its inhabitants as All Under Heaven, human beings and the spirits of nature thrive and the unseen world is very real. Emperor Shen Nung, as is the custom among the Chinese of the era, is boiling water in the shade of a *Camellia sinensis* tree. A mystic wind blows through the branches, knocking a few leaves into the Emperor's water. Rather than pouring out the water and starting fresh, the Emperor lets the leaves steep for a while and then samples the brew. Shen Nung is delighted. The drink which will one day be called tea is born.

Green tea and our favorite cup.

More than likely, this is not the way in which tea was discovered. It is a popular legend attributed to an emperor who had been known for his progressive thinking and experimental nature. On the other hand, *someone* discovered that the leaves of this certain tree steeped in boiling water made a pleasant drink. Emperor Shen Nung is as good a candidate as anyone for an ancient and mythic invention tale. But what about the more practical development of tea?

From nomadic tribes travelling southwest of the imperial border, the Chinese first learned to make a crude kind of tea. In China, however, wild tea leaves were a food long before ever becoming a beverage. Following the example of these tribes, the Chinese rolled steamed tea leaves into balls to be eaten with oil, garlic, lard, salt, and dried fish. These edible balls served as sources of quick energy, both in their nutrition content and because of the significant level of caffeine in the leaves.

In the land of Kashmir, early tea was served with the addition of red potash—which probably had nothing to do with the nutritive value of the added potassium—anise seed, and salt. People in Myanmar enjoyed *letpet*, a salad of pickled tea leaves. The people also boiled and kneaded wild tea leaves before stuffing them into hollow bamboo stalk. These stuffed stalks would be buried in order to be dug up months later and enjoyed as a delicacy. Tibetan breakfast tea was combined with barley, salt, and goat's milk butter, and then churned to a soft and thick consistency.

All of these are uses for tea understood but not necessarily recorded. 350 CE presents the earliest credible record of tea cultivation. In this year the ancient dictionary compiled by the Duke of Chou was revised to include an entry for tea. As a drink, tea was recommended as a cure for digestive and nervous disorders. The tea leaf itself could be applied as an external paste to soothe rheumatic pains.

By 500 CE, tea leaves were being formed into cakes or bricks. These were roasted to a rich reddish-brown color. The lumps of tea would be pounded into pieces and mixed with boiling water, onion, ginger, and oranges.

Tea bricks fast became a regional form of currency. Farmers and herdsmen had little use for paper money and coins. Tea, on the other hand, was its own source of value. Bricks could be both consumed and traded. The farther a tea brick traveled from the gardens of its origin, the more valuable it became.

In 450 CE a catalog of trade goods included tea for the first time along with vinegar, noodles, and cabbages. Special groves set aside for the emperor grew tea trees producing the highest quality leaves. The shift of tea from a medicinal elixir to a pleasing beverage occurred in the beginning of the sixth century. The versatility of tea caused demand to soar. A growing number of farmers set aside parts of their lands for the cultivation of tea. Finally, in 780 CE, the Chinese government imposed the first tea tax.

Tea had arrived. A metamorphosis had begun. Tea was becoming a cultural symbol. Merchants sought an author to write a book which would unite practical information and esoteric lore. Lu Yu, a foundling raised by a Buddhist priest, produced the Ch'a Ching (the *Tea Book*), a huge written work that explored the entire known world of tea.

The romantic age of tea flourished during the Sung Dynasty (960-1280 CE). At this time, ingredients such as onions and oranges were omitted so that tea might be enjoyed by itself as a delightful beverage. Emperor Hui Tsung gave generously from the royal treasury to finance the search for more kinds of tea. By this time the island nation of Japan had been emulating its giant mainland neighbor for centuries. In 794 CE the Japanese emperor built his new palace in the Chinese fashion, complete with tea gardens. The emperor created the post of Supervisor of the Tea Gardens so that tea trees would be tended properly.

Confucian Chinese influence on Japanese thought would give birth to the world's foremost homage to tea, the Japanese tea ceremony. As an example of the beauty, dignity, and importance of tea in cultural ritual, the tea ceremony reflects the reverence of both China and Japan and has no rival. At first tea was regarded more as a sacred remedy for various illnesses than as a beverage. The elevation of tea in the form of a prescribed ceremony was the work of Zen Buddhists in the sixteenth century, and is a tradition that continues into modern times.

The teahouse is a special wooden building, called *sukiya*. In the preparation room the tea master, who may be either a man or a woman and who will perform the ritual, assembles what he will need for the four hour, spiritually cleansing and socially important ritual. Generally no more than five people will join the tea master for the ceremony. As the master prepares, the participants meditate upon the coming rite.

Everyone enters the ceremony room through a low doorway. This symbolizes that all within the room are equal. Participants may remark upon any present floral arrangements or special artwork. A fire burns in a low stove. The tools lie nearby, including a bamboo tea whisk, a tea box containing the ceremonial tea or *matcha*, a tea bowl, a scoop, a kettle, and a ladle.

Reverently, the tea master begins by putting three scoops of *matcha* into the bowl. The master then ladles hot water from the kettle onto the *matcha*. This thick mixture is admired by everyone present before the master whisks it into a frothy emerald liquid. One of the kneeling participants shuffles forward and takes the bowl of tea into the palm of his left hand while supporting it with the fingers of his right hand.

Next comes enjoyment and reverence of the tea itself. The first participant takes a delicate sip and praises the flavor of the tea. That person takes two more sips before wiping the rim and passing the bowl to the next participant. After partaking of the tea, each participant wipes the rim with a napkin they have brought with them to the ceremony. When the tea has been shared by everyone, the tea master makes a second infusion to be served in individual tea cups.

Now that we have seen how tea was established in the Far East, we may legitimately wonder how tea came to Europe. For one explanation, we need to turn to India. As early as 1788, competition for land in India for the cultivation of tea was fierce in the British East India Company. Towards the middle of the nineteenth century, this British interest became the foundation on which India would become the leading tea producing nation in the world. Early on, the British had tried to grow Chinese tea trees in India without success. C.A. Bruce, a soldier and an explorer, had familiarized himself with hundreds of miles of wild Indian jungle. He knew where hundreds of wild tea trees grew—trees native to India which would thrive in Indian soil. Through his hard work, the British developed vast areas capable of bearing a rich growth of tea. Bruce's success encouraged the British government to allow private merchants access to the tea growing enterprise in India. The first shipments of native Indian tea arrived in London in 1838.

Tea had already made its way to the West well before it became a readily-available commodity. We find the first reference to tea in European sources in 1588, when the Portuguese came across the drink in their trade with China. The Dutch introduced the habit of drinking tea to sixteenth century Europe. England, the European nation most closely associated with drinking tea, got its first teas from the island of Java in 1658.

Tea drinking was by no means fashionable. Coffee and cocoa were far more trendy long before tea found its way onto the menus of European coffeehouses. By 1620, amounts of tea were shipped from Holland to France and England, reflecting a certain acceptance of the drink. In 1669, the British East India Company brought Chinese tea back to England. Within nine years, the Company was importing tea in huge quantities.

When tea first appeared in Europe, its price was extremely high. Tea was a novelty drink enjoyed by the very rich. Heavy taxes increased already tremendous prices and the result was an inevitable round of smuggling. But taxes had been greatly reduced by the eighteenth century. Tea became an affordable and popular drink—a taste of the high life in a cup. Tea has always been seen as something special. It is a drink worth savoring, a drink worth taking a pause to enjoy.

Tea comes in many types and flavors. There is sure to be a tea to suit any palate. Each has its own distinct taste and aroma. The processes of producing tea create the three categories of tea. *Green tea* is tea that has not been oxidized at all, *Oolong tea* is semi-oxidized, and *black tea* is fully oxidized. Tea is also classified as Chinese or Indian tea, even though the actual locations of tea cultivation may cover a wider area.

Black tea makes up the majority of the tea types. Assam tea is made from brittle black leaves. The tea is reddish and has a strong, brisk flavor. Excellent quality Assam tea is recognized by bright golden leaf tips.

Ceylon tea is considered as one of the finest teas in the world. Golden color and delicate aroma complement a full taste.

The Indian government has lately become especially strict about what teas may bear the name Darjeeling. This tea requires about five minutes to fully brew, but is well worth the wait. Darjeeling is a large leaf tea with a rich flavor and a fruity bouquet.

Earl Grey blends Darjeeling and Chinese tea with a little oil of bergamot. This tea is celebrated around the world for its delicate flavor. A flavor counterbalance to Earl Grey, English Breakfast is a blend of Assam and Ceylon teas and has a full-bodied flavor. Irish Breakfast, on the other hand, is made from Assam tea and is perfect for the early morning.

Fine quality teas from the Anhui province of China are called Keemum (also called Keemun) teas. These are notably less astringent than other teas and have a rich and delicate flavor. The subtle quality of Keemum makes it a wonderful tea to help people suffering from digestive problems.

The best quality Lapsang Souchong comes from Fukien province in China. This tea has an unmistakable smoky flavor—one person we know jokingly compared its flavor to smoked ham. Just the smallest bit of this tea added to another tea will lend its smokiness. Rose Pouchong comes from the southeast coast of China. The name is derived from the tradition of mixing rose petals in with the tea leaves. As a blend it is delicate and fragrant. Yunnan tea comes from the remote Chinese province of the same name. This tea is a deep golden color with a sweet flavor.

There are two types of Oolong tea. Formosa is one of the best and most expensive teas in the world. The best of these large brown leaves can be identified by silver tips. The tea is pale yellow with a slight peach flavor. Pouchong tea leaves are scented with blossoms such as jasmine.

Green tea also comes in two types, Gunpowder and Jasmine. Gunpowder is the most popular green tea in the West. Its leaves make a straw colored, fruity flavored drink. Jasmine tea is a blend of green and black teas with jasmine blossoms.

We end our discussion of tea with a brief look at the history of tea in the New World. It is believed that tea was brought to the Dutch colony of New Amsterdam from Holland in about 1650. The habit of tea drinking turned popular after New Amsterdam passed into British hands in 1674 and became New York. English colonists took the habit of tea drinking with them to many countries including Australia and New Zealand as well as to South Africa.

In 1765 Britain began to tax its American colonies without their consent, imposing a small tax of three pence a pound on tea. The colonists were infuriated. When the first three tea ships arrived at Boston a band of men dressed in Native American garb descended on the ships during the night of December 16, 1773. This was the famous "Boston Tea Party" when colonists threw 342 chests of tea into the sea. War was inevitable, and the American Revolution was the outcome.

With the abolition of the British East India Company's monopoly in 1874, merchants began to look for quicker means of transport. The Company's cumbersome ships simply were not fast enough to meet the increasing demand. A new breed of ship built by the Americans was put on the China trading route. In 1850 Britain launched the "Stornaway." She was followed by many famous tea clippers such as the "Fiery Cross," "Flying Spur," "Flying Cloud" and the most famous of them all, the "Cutty Sark."

A simple cup of tea is much more than meets the eye. In this one beverage which we in our modern world enjoy regularly are so many different threads of history—cultivation, preparation, transportation, society, politics, economics. Tea truly is the world in your cup!

Tea Time!
hands-on adventures

We thought it would be a good idea to feature some questions and activities at the end of each chapter as a kind of review. Tea Time! will also give you a chance to reflect on what you have read. There are no right or wrong answers to the questions, and the suggested activities are just that, suggestions. You will probably come up with your own ideas for putting what you read into action. That is fine, too!

1. Did you have any ideas about tea leaf reading before you began this book? What image did the term *tasseomancy* bring up?

2. What has been your experience with tea? Are you an avid tea fan, a tea dabbler, or do you dislike the drink altogether?

3. How do you usually buy tea? Are there any specialty shops in your area featuring unusual teas? Here's a suggestion: on your next trip to the local supermarket, check out the aisle where teas are kept. Are there just boxes of tea bags, or do you also find tins of loose tea? How many brands of tea are offered? What kinds of teas are offered?

4. While you are at the supermarket, or better yet, the tea shop, take the time to read a few of the tea boxes and tea tins. Did you pick up any new information about tea? Were there details about where the tea was picked?

5. Tea is the second-most popular drink in the world, right after water. Take a look at the price-per-pound of various teas in your region. How do these prices compare with the price of coffee? Which are the most expensive teas? Do you notice a difference in price between black and green teas? Between caffeinated and decaffeinated teas?

Chapter Two

The Story of Tasseomancy

Tasseomancy has a history that predates the use of tea leaves in fortune telling rites. Keep in mind that "tasseomancy" literally is divination through the use of a cup or a bowl. *Where* the shapes to be read land in the vessel is what yields information. Whether that material is a fine Earl Grey or a wild boiled bark basically makes no difference.

While there is no absolute proof that early man practiced tasseomancy, what we do know gives strong evidence that this was the case. Bowls and bowl-shaped objects have been uncovered around the world and in the areas of the earliest human habitation. Divination is certainly as old as humanity itself. Given the inclination in human nature to seek meaning in symbols, it is not hard to imagine early human beings figuring out some system of tasseomancy. At its essential level, tasseomancy is a method of divination that appeals to the primal mind.

The first records of discernable tasseomancy come from the cultures of Sumeria. For the early civilisations of the Fertile Crescent, the cultivation and brewing of a beer-like beverage from barley was a cultural staple. At this time, a woman had a choice of two professions. She could go to the temple and become a sacred prostitute, a career choice which had no kind of negative social stigma and in fact was considered a holy vocation. But if she felt more like having an active role in the everyday life of her world, she could become the Sumerian equivalent of a bartender, which also would require her to brew the barley drink she sold.

More often than not, barley beer could not be well filtered. Bits of barley would float in the drink. Records from the cities of Kish and Lagash suggest that beer mistresses would often offer to tell their customers' fortune using the barley in the beer. What system they may have used is lost to time, but there are hints that the readings were based on the location of the barley clinging to the inside surface of the drinking vessel.

There is also evidence that the Sumerians looked into their future with cups of boiled bark. Medicinal beverages made with herbs were examined for what the residual plant matter might impart about the illness at hand. Similar practices existed in Egyptian and Phoenician cultures.

When the Sumerians were first examining bits of barely in their beer cups, tea had not yet come into its own in China. However, the people still sought for ways to gain the wisdom and visions of their ancestors. Berries of various kinds were readily available. People would boil a handful of berries in a ritually special metal pot as an offering to the ancestors. Later, when the skin had peeled away from the berries and the berries themselves broke apart, the residue would be used in combination with the bowl of the pot to tell the fortunes of the people involved.

Among the ancient Greeks, the leaf of the bay laurel tree was believed to have strong prophetic powers. We are most familiar with the Pythian Oracle at Delphi, who inhaled the fragrant smoke of burning bay leaves before giving her prophecies in the name of Apollo, the god who was said to give the Pythia her visions. People who could not make the trek to Delphi could still use the energy of bay leaves, provided adequate homage was made to Apollo. An Athenian blacksmith, for example, could take a few bay leaves and boil them in water. Rather than a cup or a similar small vessel, this process involved using a large bowl. For greatest effectiveness, our blacksmith would crumble up dried leaves or tear fresh leaves into smaller pieces. Drinking the resulting brew itself can put a person into a more prophetic mindset, but we mention this only for your edification; drinking a brew of bay leaves is not recommended. The real prophecy came from the various symbols and suggestions made by the bay leaves within the bowl. In later history, the Persians borrowed this divination practice from the Greeks, spreading it throughout the Persian Empire and beyond.

The Romans regarded the bay leaf readings with smug interest. It was a quaint thing to have a plant tell the future. But the Roman Empire had its own gods and its own methods of divination, namely to read the future from the entrails of a sacrificed animal. This is the official view at any rate. Doubtless, other less elaborate means of reading were practiced by the people. The rise of Christianity in the Roman world made divination of any sort suspicious behavior. An ancient paradigm of gods interacting with man was slowly being replaced by a monotheism in which fortune telling was taboo.

But the ancient ways were alive and well in Northern Europe. We found no record of Celtic peoples practicing anything like tasseomancy, yet the concept seems to have been strongly embraced in Scandinavia. These lands in the warm seasons of the year yield a bounty of flowers and herbs which the people used for all kinds of purposes. In Scandinavia, tasseomancy was taken to a new level. Not only were herbs used for fortune telling, specific herbs would be used for specific question topics such as love or health.

In the Medieval period the Church scorned all methods of divination. Getting caught in the act of fortune telling could have dire consequences for the guilty party. Taking this into consideration, it is no wonder that the practice of reading into the future did not enjoy the outward popularity that it had gained in the ancient world. Human nature being what it is, people of Medieval Europe did not just abandon these practices. They took their divination underground.

No one method can be said to have been popular in this time period. However, records of a practice with a kinship to tasseomancy have come down to us through the centuries. The practitioners were for the most part blacksmiths, therefore having access to the tools. An individual would take a bucket or a kettle and fill it with water. Then they would take some molten metal—usually iron—and drizzle it into the water. The reader would then make what they could out of what they saw.

The Renaissance brought a new tolerance for fortune telling to Europe. From the sixteenth century onwards, Western Europe became the new home for the renowned wandering people, the Romany. This introduced a new cultural element into countries and peoples just waking up from the Dark Ages. As a people, the Romany had their own culture, their own cosmology, their own history, and their own traditions. Tea remained a strange custom to Europeans but was very much a part of Romany life. Especially in England, the Romany brought their practices of tea drinking and tasseomancy to the nobility, who would sneak away to have their leaves read by skilled Romany.

By the late eighteenth and early nineteenth centuries, fascinated English people had discovered that by studying what the Romany could do with tea leaves, they themselves could not only read leaves but could throw grand parties centered around a tasseomancy session. In Victorian England, it was fashionable, although still perceived as considerably naughty, to throw a tea party using the very best dishes and silver where the host or hostess would read the guests' tea leaves.

All of this brings us to tasseomancy in recent history and in our modern culture. For the most part the prejudice against fortune telling has been dispelled, even if many people still look askance at the whole activity. Books like this one exist to show people how to read tea leaves for themselves. There are also many websites that offer similar information. Readers using Tarot cards, runes, and palmistry sometimes include tasseomancy in their repertoire. And, of course, there is a wealth of information on the website for this book, **www.worldinyourcup.com**.

Our experience has revealed that most people would not consider getting serious about tasseomancy for many reasons. The practice can be messy. It has an old-fashioned air about it. It is too hard. It is too involved. It does not make any sense. One of our goals in this book is to show how interesting and rewarding tasseomancy really is. While it is true that something more may be required, we have also seen that the reward is worth the effort.

This brief history has shown how humanity has been looking into a vessel for a glimpse of the future since our earliest age, how humanity has kept up the practice era after era, and how tasseomancy holds a place even today. Tasseomancy and humanity have come through thousands of years together, and it is our hope that this book will continue that ancient legacy.

Tea Time!
hands-on adventures

1. What have you heard about various kinds of divination? Perhaps you could check the Internet or a library and take a look at the subject.

2. Reading the Tarot is an example of cartomancy. Have you ever had a reading? What are your opinions of the Tarot? What can you find out about this method of divination?

3. A pendulum and a Ouija board are two other kinds of divination. Perhaps you, or someone you know, will have access to a Ouija board. Why not try it out and see how it works for you? You could also tie a weight to a string and hold it over a piece of paper with various answers (such as "yes, no, maybe") written on it. Let the all-knowing pendulum work for you!

4. Try making a "tea" out of a culinary herb rather than tea leaves. You could use mint or basil. How is the experience of sipping one of these teas different from that of drinking tea made from our friend *Camellia sinensis*?

5. Try mentioning tasseomancy to some of your family and friends. Do you get knowing looks or blank stares? What seems to be the prevailing opinion about divination where you live? Why are some people against all forms of divination?

Chapter Three

Brewing
Teas

As we were bringing together material for this book, we searched through our family records for any information about tea and tea leaf reading. We mentioned previously that several ladies in the family had practiced a sort of parlor tasseomancy, strictly for amusement as they had always insisted. While reading through the contents of an old trunk we came upon a tea journal penned by our great—and great-great—grandmother Grace.

The black ink Grace used had oxidized to reddish brown, but the crisp flowing letters of her ornate penmanship were as legible as when they had first been written. *Le Monde dans la Tasse*, Grace entitled her journal, *The World in the Cup*. Grace had been educated and considered French the most suitable language for her writing. We now had the title for our book, one firmly planted in our family history.

Samples of tea: Special Gunpowder Green (front & last row); Oolong, Green and Bigelow Earl Grey (middle).

Grace subtitled her journal *comment lire dans les feuilles de thé*, "how to read tea leaves." We expected to find information about doing readings, but the journal started with Grace's choices for tea throughout the day.

Apparently, she kept notes on the various teas she had enjoyed, much the way a wine connoisseur would jot down impressions of different vintages. We thought it might be interesting to share Grace's top picks from over one hundred years ago along with her hand-penned comments.

- **Breakfast:**
  Earl Grey, "a blend of teas scented with fruit of bergamot"
  English Breakfast, "full-bodied and brisk, a wake up tea"

- **Elevenses** *(late morning pick-me-ups):*
  Darjeeling, "a delicate tea with a distinct muscatel flavor, will not spoil lunch"
  Prince of Wales, "a bright tea combining the character of Keemun with a hint of Oolong"

- **Afternoon:**
  Darjeeling, "excellent after lunch as well as before"
  Java Green Tea, "a light brew, quite mellow, excellent in the heat"
  Lapsang Souchong, "a smoky tea with strong flavor, excellent in cold weather"

- **After Dinner:**
  Earl Grey, "excellent at both ends of the day, best with milk, must be kept closely sealed"
  Green Tea & Mint, "a soothing blend of green tea and peppermint, an excellent digestive"
  Gunpowder Green, "another delicate tea, straw-colored and thirst-quenching"

- **Evening:**
  Blackcurrant/Apple, "the richness of blackcurrants blended with the sweetness of apple, a gentle drink"
  Jasmine, "a fragrant tea, light colored, gentle"

- **Night:**
  Chamomile and Apple, "delicate chamomile flavor with apple and cinnamon, a spicy tasting drink, relaxing"
  Gunpowder Green, "a delicate, straw-colored, thirst-quenching"
  Jasmine, "also good late at night for its gentle properties"

Grace went on to note that the *Gunpowder* teas were good for doing readings, as were *Earl Grey* and *Darjeeling*. "The *Lapsang Souchong*," she noted, "gives a pleasant and useful distribution of leaves, but its strong flavor distracts from the reading. Guests are so full of comments about the smoky nature of the tea that they scarcely attend to what the leaves are revealing."

Our (great-) great grandmother's selections encouraged us in our quest for teas to recommend in this book. It says a lot about the world of tea that each blend Grace favored is still available today. We tried all of the above teas and found Grace's brief summaries to be accurate and reliable. The blackcurrant/apple blend was wonderful hot, a dessert in itself, but it was outstanding served as a cold beverage. Our guests never believed it was a kind of flavored ice tea.

So, you may be thinking, what could possibly be special about brewing a cup of tea? You take a tea bag, put it into a cup, and add hot water. Simple and straightforward, right?

Well, this is adequate if you just want a fast cup of tea in the morning. But this book is not about taking quick sips on the go. Tasseomancy elevates brewing tea to an art form. In tasseomancy, no one part of the creation of tea does not affect the whole. Brewing the tea used in readings with reverence is as important as the reading itself. If you consider tea as only flavored leaves in water, you may as well try to do a reading using powdered fruit punch. Tea is the result of the brewing process, containing the energies set free as hot water releases the delicate flavors held in the leaves.

Bear in mind that brewing tea for tasseomancy should not be a mundane task as might be making tea for usual consumption. You should achieve and maintain the mindset that you are doing special work. Be aware of the rich process that is brewing.

We have found great success in applying a paradigm based on the traditional elements of Western magic. These are Earth, Water, Fire, and Air. Is it necessary to use a kind of pattern like this? It is not necessary, but it is extremely effective. This approach has enabled us to observe the brewing process in each of its parts as well as in the entirety. Thus while we are suggesting the elemental paradigm, feel free to adapt whatever system works best for you.

Earth is represented by the tea itself. Tea plants take root in soil and go on to grow and flourish. The earth is the mother and the nurturer of tea. It only seems logical to us to associate the leaves with the earth element.

Now onto the tea and to the forms in which it is available. Most of us are familiar with the tea bag. In fact, it was the invention of the tea bag that revolutionized tea drinking, as dropping a tea bag into a cup of water is so much easier than measuring out loose tea into an infuser. Suddenly, tea could be enjoyed in minutes—just add water. There is always a question about the grade of tea found in tea bags and loose tea. We discovered that the leaves put into bags were actually the broken remains of loose tea. But this does not make the bag tea any less useful or enjoyable. We will be showing you how to use tea bags for emergency readings.

Loose tea is usually available in specialty shops. A growing number of supermarkets are offering loose tea, and tea of superb quality has always been available in neighborhood ethnic shops. How you can acquire loose tea will depend upon where you live. Essentially a box of loose tea is sold according to weight instead of being parceled out into servings like teabags. For tasseomancy, you will probably prefer to use loose tea. After all, readings are made from the patterns of leaves against the inverted dome of the teacup.

As we have mentioned, there are many varieties of tea on the market. Which are the best for tasseomancy? What kinds of readings—for instance, finances or family concerns—are best done with what kinds of tea? To be practical, any kind of black tea will suit all purposes. But if you want to put a little extra effort into it, there are some teas that will enhance certain readings.

For our part, we favor using green tea for our readings. This is really a matter of our own preference. However, other tasseomancers we have spoken to say that green tea is especially good for readings involving the human spirit. One example would be when doing readings for guests who do not feel in harmony with the universe around them. What could help? Let the leaves reveal a solution.

Black tea is probably the most widely used tea in tasseomancy. One reason might be that the dark leaves are easier to read and patterns are more pronounced. Think of black tea as the tea for concrete issues and questions. Now let us consider the tea bag and its place in tasseomancy. Using a tea bag is simple enough. Brew your reading cup of tea to suit your taste. After drinking enough so that only a quarter inch of liquid is left in the cup, open the bag and let the leaves float free. You might want to stir the mixture with a teaspoon before turning the cup over. Proceed with your reading as you would with any other mixture.

You may be thinking that using a tea bag will render a less than quality reading. This is not the case. Tea really is tea, whether in a bag or in an infuser. We may be suggesting a more ornate ceremony to accompany your readings, but never underestimate the usefulness of the quick bag reading.

While doing research for this book, we decided to look into the kinds of teas that were readily available in our local market. We had tried all kinds of supermarket teabags and now we wanted to see how various loose teas compared. Of course, we were not primarily interested in *tasting* the teas; we wanted to see if there were any differences in the kinds of readings we would get.

The Spice Corner has been a fixture in Philadelphia's Ninth Street Market for decades. It is a small store crammed with all kinds of spices, coffees and kitchen accessories. There is also a whole aisle dedicated to a wide variety of teas. Hundreds of glass containers, each one carefully hand-labeled to indicate the tea inside, line the shelves on both sides.

We waited patiently, ducking under hanging spices and tea equipment, for our turn with a salesperson. The store was filled with people and it was almost ten minutes before Tina turned to us.

"We're looking for a variety of loose teas," I said. "What's your most popular seller?"

"Earl Grey," Tina said, walking us up the aisle to where three containers of the tea sat. "It's $3.25 a quarter."

"And for a half-pound?"

Tina looked at the label on the container. "$6.25," she said, "but you have to keep it tightly closed. Otherwise the bergamot oil will evaporate."

"We'll take a quarter-pound," my partner said.

Tina filled a plastic bag with approximately four ounces of tea. She weighed the bag on an old-fashioned scale, added a bit more tea with a plastic scoop and closed the bag with a twist tie.

"Anything else?"

"Yes, actually," I answered. "We're here to get a variety of loose teas. We'd like your advice on how to select a wide range."

"How will you use the tea?"

"We're going to do some tea leaf readings."

Tina smiled at this. She turned and led us down a different narrow aisle. "I have just the thing: Imperial Gunpowder. A lot of people use plain black tea for readings, but I think Gunpowder leaves cling to the side of the cup better."

She reached up and brought down a glass container filled with grayish tea leaves that were tightly curled into tiny balls. The tea was $14.95 a pound, $7.50 a half and $3.95 a quarter. As we requested, Tina measured out a quarter-pound into a plastic bag. For now, we were buying small quantities so we could try a lot of teas.

"Do you do readings?" my partner asked Tina.

"No, not me personally, but my roommate does. I've learned something of the art by watching her."

"And what kind of tea does your roommate prefer?"

"Cheryl likes to use green tea. She says it's more healthful."

"Okay, I guess we should try some green tea, then," I said.

Tina showed us seven containers with different kinds and qualities of green tea. The prices were all within about fifteen cents of each other so we had to ask a lot of questions to find out what the differences were.

"I think it depends on your own preferences," Tina explained. "This green, for example, has a slightly smoky taste that some people like and others hate."

We picked up two green teas, a bit of *Russian Gold* and a little *Lapsang Souchong*. Tina walked us up to one of the cash registers in the front of the store.

"Good luck with your readings," she said as she turned and began to help another customer.

We know that not every town and city has a *Spice Corner*, so we checked on the Internet for good places to buy teas. There are a lot of them!

Three reliable sources that we found and ordered from are the well known Bigelow (www.bigelowtea.com), the Tea Guys (www.theteaguys.com) and Adagio Teas (www.adagio.com).

Bigelow offers tea, teapots and other tea supplies. Their site has a lot of information and places to check out special offers and promotions.

The Tea Guys also has a lot of information on its site. For the ultimate in cool, they will mark your tea with a private label, as long as you buy at least one case.

Adagio Teas has a wonderful site, filled with tea lore, information and photos. Everything is clearly labeled and navigating the site is easy.

If you cannot find the tea you want locally, we encourage you to give one of these sites a try. Or you can always use Google (www.google.com), type in "tea," "loose tea," or "gourmet tea" and hunt down your own site. If you enjoy drinking tea, these online merchants are a good way to expand your experience.

We cannot have tea without water. As you might expect, the element of Water is represented by water itself. Water is the soothing, stable elemental factor. It is the medium of insight and inspiration. All of the mystic qualities of water are infused into the tea during the brewing process.

What kind of water provides the best readings? This is not a frivolous question as there are many kinds of water available. Some readers we know swear by natural spring water. For us, we have never had a problem using water straight from the tap. Perhaps this seems a bit ordinary, but for city folk like us the tap is akin to going down to the river or the well to fetch water. And our local city water is of excellent quality.

Here is one note about the de-ionized water that you can probably find in your supermarket. We fail to see the point in paying good money for water that has had something removed. The same would go for distilled water. If you would like to use either of these, by all means use your own judgement. For us, we feel that not only are these waters a waste of money, they also lack a certain living energy.

Joseph F. Conroy & Emilie J. Conroy

Fire is the element of transformation. This is physically evident when we see wood change to ashes in a fire. Fire transforms the wood or gas into heat. In brewing tea, it is heat that transforms leaves and water into a finely flavored beverage.

Now what can we possibly say about heating water? In tasseomancer lore, the way water boils does matter. You will want to heat your water completely, bringing it to a full, rolling boil. As soon as the water reaches this stage you must remove it from the transformative element of fire. This will prevent the water from losing too much oxygen. Water with too little oxygen will make a flat, dull tea.

Tea is the end result of a process of immersion and combination, of Earth and Water uniting through the heat of Fire. The element of Air, then, is the finished product, the tea that will be used for readings. Air is the union of the other three elements and is the intellectually-charged result in which is contained wisdom

The union of Earth, Water, and Fire results in the finished product of tea. For us, we represent this totality with the element of Air. This may seem like a random assignment of the remaining element, but in reality you might consider Air the most important component. Air embraces the intellect and energy of the practitioner in the endeavor of a tea leaf reading. Air allows Fire to burn. Air is present in Water and Earth.

Most of the tea experts we spoke with recommended similar steps for making a perfect cup of tea. Of course, a perfect cup of tea is an essential for the ambience of a leaf reading, and as a mood setter, amber tea filling a delicate white cup cannot be surpassed.

Begin with freshly drawn cold water. Check to see that your kettle or other water boiling apparatus and your teapots are spotlessly clean and free of any residue from previous uses. Warm the teapots with hot water, then rinse out the water.

Use the suggested number of tea bags. If you are using loose tea, figure on a teaspoon of tea per cup. The yield in cups of tea will depend upon the volume of the teapot. A 20-ounce teapot will serve two people, for example.

Bring your water to a fresh boil. This will be water best suited to making good tea. Water that has been boiled, allowed to cool, and then boiled again will yield a flat-tasting tea. Too much oxygen has been removed from the water.

Add the water to the tea in the teapot. Let the tea brew for three to five minutes. Stir the tea to distribute the flavor adequately. Pour the tea into your guests' cups and allow them to sweeten or add milk as suits them.

If you are doing an afternoon reading and want to create a special ambience, you might want to consider offering light refreshments along with the tea. These could range from the traditional cream cheese and cucumber tea sandwiches to an assortment of cookies. Having exceptional snacks will enhance the significance of the afternoon's activities in the minds of your guests and querents.

On the simple side, you could set out the fanciest plate you have with varied cookies. The beauty of the plate will serve to accentuate the offering, even if your cookies are store-bought. You might even have seen that ubiquitous blue tin of Royal Dansk cookies and decide to offer those, appropriately displayed on a tray or three-tiered serving dish.

In case you want to make the event really special, we rummaged about in our family recipe binders just to find something distinctive for you to serve to your guests. We found the following two recipes from France.

■ *Tuile* is the French word for tile, you know, the red-orange half-pipe tiles one sees everywhere in the south of France. Tuiles are crisp, delicious cookies shaped like those tiles. The ones we have here are called *tuiles à l'orange*. They have an orange and almond flavor. They are not overly difficult to make—if you follow our instructions—and are uncommon enough to delight your guests. The recipe below will yield about a dozen tuiles, depending on size and thickness.

Ingredients:

1/3 cup orange juice (Freshly squeezed is a gourmet touch.)
Zest of one large orange

1/4 cup Grand Marnier
(Yes, you really need this, but don't worry, the alcohol will cook off in the baking.)
1 1/4 cups granulated white sugar
7 tablespoons unsalted butter, melted
2 cups finely chopped sliced almonds
1 cup sifted all-purpose flour

Note: For diabetics and others who must restrict their sugar intake, a product such as Splenda may replace the sugar in the recipe.

Equipment:

large cookie sheets (at least two, but four would be convenient)
one large mixing bowl
pastry brush
table fork
one teaspoon
one small bowl of water
rolling pin
spatula
cooling rack

Method:

Dip a pastry brush in the melted unsalted butter and coat a cookie sheet with it. The cookie sheet must be well greased or the tuiles will stick to it. Place your oven rack in the center of the oven and preheat the oven to 350°F. In a large mixing bowl, combine all the ingredients. The result will be a fairly stiff dough. Let the mixture rest, uncovered, for ten to fifteen minutes. When you come back to the dough, use a teaspoon to scoop out a portion of the mixture. Drop the teaspoon of dough onto the cookie sheet. Dip the table fork into some water and use it to press the portion of dough into a thin round shape. Keep wetting your fork in the bowl of water and continue to scoop out dough and press it into shape on the cookie sheet. The dough should be about the thickness of an almond, so it is important to press the mixture well. You should put no more than four cookies on each cookie sheet. The cookies will spread as they bake.

Bake until the cookies are golden brown, about seven minutes. Rotate the cookie sheets during this time, moving them from front to back to be sure the cookies are baking evenly. While this batch is baking, you can prepare the next sheets.

Before you remove the cookies from the oven, have a spatula and rolling pin ready. Take the cookie sheets from the oven and allow to cool for about a half-minute or so. You want to be able to lift them off the sheet without tearing them, so they have to be elastic. Using the spatula, place each cookie on top of the rolling pin and press it gently into a curved—tile-like—shape   Continue in the same way with the other cookies.

Because the universe is not filled with perfect moments, sometimes the cookies will become too stiff to mold over the rolling pin. If this happens, return them to the oven very briefly. When the cookies are molded, transfer them to a cooling rack.

Tuiles are best eaten the day they are made. You can save the batter in the refrigerator for the next day if you need another batch. It has been our experience that leftover tuiles are never a problem: they tend to disappear quickly!

■ A *clafoutis* ("klah-foo-TEE") is a pie-shaped cake made from batter poured over fruit. This is another treat-with-tea that will make your guests feel special. Originally from the Limousin region of France, a clafoutis is traditionally made with cherries, often not pitted in the old-fashioned recipes. We recommend pitted cherries.

Ingredients:

3 cups pitted cherries (fresh or drained from can)
1 1/4 cup milk
2/3 cup sugar
3 eggs
2 teaspoons vanilla
pinch of salt
1/2 cup flour
1/4 cup powdered sugar
1/4 cup melted unsalted butter
2 tablespoons kirschwasser or cognac

Note: Once again, Splenda or the like can be used to replace the sugar in the recipe.

Equipment:

blender
large, deep oven-proof pie dish
sieve
pastry brush

Method:

Preheat oven to 350°F. Add milk, sugar, eggs, vanilla, salt and flour together in a blender and puree until smooth. Add the kirschwasser or cognac and blend again for 15 seconds. Using the pastry brush, spread unsalted butter on the bottom and sides of the large pie dish.

Spread cherries evenly in the dish. Pour the batter over the top gently. Bake on middle rack of oven for 45-50 minutes, until top is brown. Insert a knife into the middle of the pie dish to see if the clafoutis is done. The knife will come out clean. Remove from oven. Place powdered sugar in a sieve and sprinkle over top of the clafoutis. Serve immediately.

You may substitute other seasonal fruits for the cherries. We have used blueberries, apples, and pears. With very juicy fruit, you will have to increase the amount of flour in the recipe from 1/2 cup to 2/3 cup. When we made a clafoutis with peaches, we used 1 1/4 cups of flour. If you wish, you can omit the kirschwasser or cognac. You could also use a small dash of almond extract. When serving, slice the clafoutis into thin wedges.

We have now covered the territory of brewing tea, explored the elemental significance of the brewing process and given you some ideas for holding a special afternoon tea. Before you try a tea leaf reading, we suggest you take some time to know and understand brewing as the union of Earth, Water, Fire, and Air. Feel the tea leaves between your fingertips and think of Earth. Gaze into the clarity of Water and think of your own insight and inspiration. Watch the graceful dance of Fire and think of this transformation from leaf to beverage. Finally, think of Air and of the energies you will need to make successful tea readings. By Earth, Water, Fire, and Air, you have the ability to read the leaves. Keep reading to gain the knowledge.

Tea Time!
hands-on adventures

1. Why not go out and sample several of the teas mentioned in this chapter? You might want to try a sampler box so you can get the greatest variety in small quantities for this experiment. Perhaps you will want to keep brief notes about the teas you try and your reactions to them.

2. What kind of tea brewing equipment do you already have? What styles do you have? What would you like that you do not have?

3. Do you already have a favorite tea? What is it that you like about this tea? Or are all teas pretty much the same to you? Why not pick out one completely new tea that you have not tried in the other experiment and try it now?

4. Do you have a tradition of tea drinking in your family or life? Where do you think the occasional tea leaf reading will fit in?

5. Now that you have tried a variety of teas, how about try different styles. Take, for example, an Earl Grey. Try making a cup from a regular teabag, then try a cup made from loose tea. Do you notice any differences? If you are really adventurous, you could also try making a cup from whole-leaf tea. It might be difficult to find, but we think you will find the experience interesting.

Chapter Four

Growing
Your Own Tea

The phone rings.

"Hello, Dad? Emilie here."

"Yes, Emilie?"

"How do you feeling about growing our own tea?"

"I don't know anything about it. Can we get tea plants? And will they grow where we live?

"I'm here in the South and you're up there in the Northeast, so we have different climates, and there will be different problems, but, yes, I think we can actually grow tea plants!"

"Okay, let's give it a try then."

"I'm glad you agree. I've already ordered five plants for each of us. Yours should be there in about a week."

And that is how, in the middle of research on tea leaf reading, both of the authors became involved in trying to nurse toddler tea plants into healthy, mature shrubs. We both enjoy gardening and were ready to tackle what we thought would be tricky, fussy, difficult to grow specimens. To our surprise, once we met some basic needs of the plant such as soil quality, temperature and moisture, the tea seedlings grew eagerly and without much struggle on our part.

If you, too, enjoy gardening, you might want to try growing your own tea plants. That is why we have included this chapter, detailing the essential information about selecting, planting, growing and harvesting tea. Even if you do not think it likely that you will be caring for tea plants, the information we provide here will give you a clearer understanding of what tea is, where it comes from, and what words such as green, oolong and black mean in the tea world.

Before you can do a tea leaf reading, you need tea. Fortunately, tea is one of the most readily available commodities in the world. Obtaining tea leaves can be as easy as a trip to the local supermarket. There, in the tea and coffee aisle, you can select a convenient box of tea bags, choose from among the specialty teas, or perhaps find loose tea in canisters.

Some people will prefer to go to a spice shop or a tea specialty store where varieties of loose tea abound. They can buy a pound, half-pound, or even a few ounces. Occasionally, tea fanciers will find whole-leaf tea for sale. This is the complete tea leaf, not cut or chopped.

A quick trip online will reveal many dealers selling mail order teas and equipment. The selection is broad, the prices are generally good, and delivery rapid. Tea is an eminently transportable commodity.

And for those of us who like to garden, there is a new option: growing our own tea plants. This is an excellent procedure for those who want to participate in the entire process of tea leaf reading from growing and picking the leaves themselves to preparing the brew and inspecting the leaves in the bottom of the cup.

Several nurseries now offer authentic tea plants. In our research, we typed "tea plants" into search engines and found a number of places offering tea plants. **Live Herb Nursery**, for example, charges ten dollars for a tea plant in a four-inch pot. The address is 155 Elm Forest Loop, Cedar Creek, Texas, 78612, the telephone number is (512) 303-4505, and the e-mail address is liveherbnursery@aol.com for inquiries and orders.

One of the widest selections of plants is offered by **Camellia Forest Nursery**, 9701 Carrie Road, Chapel Hill, North Carolina, 27516, telephone (919) 968-0504, e-mail camforest@aol.com and web site http://www.cam-forest.com/ for further information and photos.

This nursery offers *Camellia sinensis* in large-leaf form (winter hardy to zone 7A or 8). This shrub has large and leathery leaves, with a multi-branched trunk growing to about fifteen feet. White, cup-shaped blooms begin to appear as early as August. The price per plant depends on the size of the plant and runs from twelve to thirty-five dollars.

The same nursery also has pink-flowered tea plants with pale pink flowers from sixteen to eighteen dollars per plant, and a true Chinese variety (*Camellia sinensis* variety *sinensis*) featuring tea plants grown from Chinese seed priced at ten to eighteen dollars per plant.

If you would prefer to grow a Japanese-style tea plant, Camellia Forest Nursery has a small-leaf variety widely cultivated in Japan priced at ten to thirty-five dollars per plant depending on size.

As a third example of sources for tea plants, we found **Nichols Garden Nursery**, 1190 Old Salem Road NE, Albany, Oregon, 97321-4580, telephone 1 (800) 422-3985. The nursery has an informative web site at http://www.nicholsgardennursery.com/, and charges around twenty-six dollars for each plant.

Commercially, tea is grown on large plantations around the world. It is a labor-intensive activity since harvesting tea still requires hand-picking of the tender shoots. For our purposes, we will assume that you, like us, do not intend to create a tea plantation. We will present an overview of how to grow and harvest tea in a garden or in a container.

All varieties of tea plants belong to the same genus and species, camellia sinensis, with different varieties found in various countries. These are evergreen shrubs with white cup-shaped flowers that have yellow stamens. The plants can grow to tree height, seven or eight feet. They are generally kept trimmed at two to five feet in height to make harvesting the leaves easier. The young leaves are the source of the best tea.

Tea plants are in the same genus as the *camellia*. They are surprisingly easy to grow. Being evergreens, the plants will produce tea leaves all year long, and flowers from March to May. The flowers are fragrant and will be most abundant if pollinated by bees. The plants prefer partial shade and need well drained soil.

Tea plants are hardy to Zone 8, tolerating temperatures as low as fifteen to twenty degrees if protected. Beyond Zone 8, tea plants would have to be grown in a hothouse. The plants prefer a humid summer with lots of rainfall. They also like a cool, dry winter with no frost. In colder climates, where frost and freezing are common, tea plants can be kept inside from late fall until early spring.

People who grow tea plants find them highly ornamental, with beautiful deep green leaves. The shoots, which include the bud and two tender leaves at the end of each branch, can be picked every seven to fourteen days. Four pounds of leaves will yield one pound of dried tea.

Tea plants will do best in light to medium loam soils that are well-drained. The plants prefer acid soils with a pH between 4.5 and 5.6. When growing tea plants in containers, it is best to use potting soil made from sphagnum peat. Well composted pine bark with vermiculite added will also be suitable.

As the plants begin to put out new leaves, they should be fertilized with azalea or *Miracid* plant food. This will keep the soil acid as well as stimulate growth. When the plants are well established, they should be mulched heavily. Any pruning should be done only after the plants have flowered.

Once the plants are growing well, it will be time to begin harvesting the leaves. Pick the very young leaves and leaf buds. Do not pick the older, tougher leaves. Once the plants are three years old, the harvesting can continue throughout the growing season.

The top two leaves and the bud of the tea plant are picked from the end of the small branch and then dried. It is often hard to believe that all great tasting teas come from the same plant. The differences in flavor from, say, a green tea and a black tea is in the way the leaf is processed.

There are three major kinds of processed tea: green, oolong and black. Each of these is prepared in a different way. For the beginner, the green tea method is probably the easiest. Here is how we prepare tea leaves for green tea:

1. Pick the tender young leaves from the ends of the tea plant branches. These will usually be on young shoots with two to three leaves. Place the shoots in the shade to dry for several hours. If there is any water on the leaves, be sure this has dried up as well.

2. There will be enzymes in the tea leaves which cause oxidation. To destroy these—a necessary step—steam the leaves in a steamer on the range or cooktop for just under one minute. The water should be at a boil when you put the leaves in the steamer. Do not allow the leaves to touch the boiling water.

3. After step two, the leaves must be dried in an oven at 250 degrees Fahrenheit for about twenty minutes. By doing this, you will remove all moisture from the leave. This will stop the growth of mold and the beginning of fermentation.

4. Once the leaves have been dried, you may add flavorings if you wish. Green tea has a delicate flavor, so you would not want to add anything too strong. A bit of dried jasmine or a small amount of dried blackberry leaf will yield a delicately fruity tea. Of course, you may prefer, as we do, to enjoy the basic flavor of the green tea in its natural state.

5. Store the leaves in an airtight container. Oxidation, also referred to as "fermentation" in tea-growing circles, is the enemy of pure tea taste.

Oolong tea occupies a place between green and black tea. It is made from tea leaves that have been allowed to ferment for a brief time. When speaking of the tea-making process, "fermentation" means crumbling and exposing the tea leaves to the air. This process yields a richer, stronger tasting tea. To make an oolong-style tea from your freshly-picked leaves, follow this method:

1. Spread the shoots out in a thin layer on a mat or towel, either on the ground or on a picnic table. You want to keep the leaves from contact with the earth or table top. You should choose a sunny spot because the leaves will be left to wilt for thirty minutes to an hour. The hotter the day, the less time it should take for the leaves to wilt.

2. Once the leaves have wilted, take them inside and place them in a dark room for about four hours. Once each hour, gently stir the leaves by hand. As the time goes by, you should notice the edges of the leaves turning red. This is a sign of oxidation. The leaves will lose another twenty percent of their moisture during this process and develop the characteristic aroma and color of oolong tea.

3. After the four hours, dry the leaves in an oven set at 250 degrees Fahrenheit for about fifteen to twenty minutes. This will stop the chemical changes occurring in the leaves and fix the oolong quality in your tea.

Black tea is made from tea leaves that have gone through a fermentation process before being dried. These teas have the strongest flavors and require the longest time to produce.

1. Pick tender young shoots with two to three leaves. Place the shoots on drying racks for ten to twenty hours to get rid of any water on the surface

of the leaves. This process will reduce the internal moisture of the leaves by about seventy percent. Drying the leaves will make them more malleable for the fermentation process.

2. Once the leaves have dried, separate them from the stems. Now it is time to "bruise" the leaves. Take several leaves and roll them between your two hands, crushing them until the leaves darken and become crinkled. Doing this will begin the fermentation process by allowing more of the leaf surface to come into contact with the air. Repeat the bruising with all of the leaves you have picked. You have finished when the leaves turn a bright copper color.

3. Allow the leaves to ferment for three days. Place thin layers of leaves on a tray in a shady location. We prefer to cover the leaves with a light cheese cloth or insect netting to prevent foreign materials from mixing with the tea. After the third day of fermentation, the leaves are ready for drying.

4. Pre-heat the oven to 250 degrees Fahrenheit. Place the fermented leaves on oven-proof trays—cookie sheets, for example—and place them in the oven for twenty minutes. This process is necessary to remove the water remaining in the leaves. It will also stop the fermentation process. Heating the leaves in an oven will also seal in the flavor. After twenty minutes, the tea is ready to use. If you have made more tea than you will use immediately, store the remaining leaves in an airtight container.

Tea Time!
hands-on adventures

1. Think about your experiences in gardening. How would you rate yourself as a gardener? Do you think the idea of growing your very own tea plants is appealing? Why?

2. Will the climate where you live support tea plants? What adjustments and precautions will you have to make?

3. Can you see any benefit to growing your own tea for use in tasseomancy? Think about some non-physical influences you can have on the plants.

4. Growing tea on large plantations is labor-intensive. Can you see why? What factors keep the cost of tea from skyrocketing? Think about the labor conditions on the tea plantations.

5. Once you have picked your own leaves, what kind of tea would you like to make? Which steps seem difficult to you? What could you do to overcome this apparent difficulty?

Chapter Five

Equipment for Tea Reading

In this chapter we will look at the items that go into making and serving tea. If your goal is to read tea leaves after the tea has been drunk, then there will be a few things to keep in mind beyond the ordinary preparations.

As we did the research for this chapter, we found that practices and beliefs vary widely concerning what makes for an authentic tea leaf reading. To give you several examples of this, the following paragraphs will introduce four amateur tasseomancers who talked with us about their ways of doing a reading. We chose these four because they represent different styles and tastes.

Gloria J. considers herself a traditionalist, but on the plain side. She uses a ceramic teapot, usually white, with matching white ceramic cups and saucers. Gloria spoons loose tea into the pot and stirs the brew to make sure some leaves pour into each cup. Her guests sip the tea, and when only a bit of liquid is left, they put down the cup to allow the leaves to settle to the bottom. Gloria then has each guest turn the cup over onto the saucer, then turn it upright again. Then she examines the distribution of the leaves in the cup and begins the reading. In Gloria's readings, unadorned cups, saucers and a simple teapot are sufficient to set the stage for tasseomancy.

Mike S. became interested in tasseomancy when he was building a tea cabinet for the kitchen. His wife had many varieties of tea and often mentioned a desire for a special place to keep her collection. As Mike planned the cabinet, he began talking about reading tea leaves, something he knew his wife often did with her friends. She showed Mike how it was done, shared her notes, and he was hooked. Mike has become a formal reader; he likes to bring the tea service in on a big silver platter and includes a teapot, hot water pot, sugar, lemon slices, fancy china cups and saucers. Like Gloria, Mike also spoons loose tea into the pot. He has a special ornate teapot just for readings. In his practice, the fancy tea service emphasizes the special nature of a tea leaf reading.

Unlike Mike, Edwina M. believes in simplicity, letting all attention fall on the leaves. She uses her everyday cups and saucers, and has a "lucky" red teapot which she always uses. Unlike the others, Edwina prefers teabags, one for each cup. Each guests allows the tea to brew to taste, then removes the teabag and places it on the saucer. When just a bit of liquid remains, each guest tears open the now-cool teabag and allows the leaves to fall into the cup. Each cup is turned over, then righted, and Edwina begins the reading. Edwina says she prefers teabags because she has more leaves to work with once the cups are turned rightside up.

This tea cup is a bit narrow, but still adequate for readings; its pleasant design set the mood.

Finally we have Renée W., who was intent on showing us that tasseomancy can be performed anywhere, and with the simplest of equipment. We met Renée in a fast-food restaurant. She had several small Styrofoam cups sitting on the plastic table next to standard-issue corporate teabags. Renée had us rip open the packets and put our teabag into plain hot water from the spout next to the soda dispenser. Once we had drunk most of the tea, she told us to tear open the teabags and put the tea into the Styrofoam cup. Renée poured the little bit of remaining tea onto a pile of paper napkins, turned the cups up again, and showed us how to do a reading right then and there.

As we said, there is no one and only *right* way to do a tea leaf reading. Tasseomancy has taken different forms in other cultures and times, and remains a varied practice in our own day. The essential ingredient in each method is a good cup of tea.

Fortunately, making tea is not rocket science. Almost everyone can do it, and even those who do not cook will admit to being able to boil water. That said, there are some techniques which yield a better cup of tea than others. And whether you are making tea to enjoy the drink or to read leaves, a really good cup of tea is still an excellent idea. The quality of the tea in the cup will not alter your reading, but life is too short for us to be satisfied with indifferent beverages.

All truly wonderful cups of tea begin with two basic elements: the tea leaves and the water. In Chapter Three we talked about the different kinds of tea available. Which tea you use will probably not affect your reading, so you should select something you and your guests enjoy. As for the water, there are many opinions.

Bottled spring water usually comes to mind first when we talk about quality water. Of course, we cannot just believe that all bottled water has been drawn from a pure mountain spring by smiling workers with impeccably clean hands. Some off-the-shelf waters have been produced under factory-like conditions from modified tap water.

Other bottled waters really do come from a natural spring. The usual recommendation obtains here: read the label. Make sure you know what kind of bottled water you are buying. Pure, additive-free water in a bottle may make better tasting tea, if only because the chemicals and anti-bacterial agents found in tap water are missing.

If you are fortunate enough to live in an area where tap water is of high quality and free from odd tastes, this may be all you need to brew excellent tea. Let the water run a bit before filling your tea kettle and you will have fresher tasting tea.

Whichever kind of water you choose to use, it is important to bring it to a full rolling boil, then pour it immediately into your teapot. Do not let the water boil on and on: this will result in a flat-tasting tea.

Depending on your own traditions and preferences, tea leaf readings may occur as a pleasant diversion after a meal or afternoon tea. Or you may do your readings as a separate activity. In either case, it is a good idea to put some thought into your tea service.

Putting thought into a tea service does not necessarily mean going to a lot of expense. Renée W., whom we mentioned earlier, met us in a fast food place to talk about tea leaf readings and gave us a quick reading using only a Styrofoam cup and a standard-issue tea bag. "When you get right down to it," she said, "it's really all about the leaves in the cup. The rest is just showmanship." Even the finely-chopped leaves from corporate teabags formed patterns suitable for a reading.

Of course, in your own home you may want more of a production than Styrofoam cups and store-brand tea bags. But remember that the essence of tea leaf reading, as Renée pointed out, remains the distribution of the leaves in the cup.

In the next paragraphs we will run through the various items you could use as part of your tea leaf reading presentation. We have tried to be comprehensive, but you need not be. Pick and choose from the items below according to your needs and preferences.

If you want to do some searching and shopping online, Bigelow has a good site. Go to *http://www.bigelowtea.com* and click on "shop." Or you could visit the Twinings site at *http://www.twinings.com/en_int/index.asp* for more information about brewing and enjoying teas.

Now, on to the essential components of a good tea service. We have given a variety of choices for each item. What you use is up to you, your needs, budget and taste.

Tea Kettle

Before everything else is the tea kettle. You cannot make tea if you do not have boiled water, and a good kettle is essential. We prefer a solid metal kettle, usually stainless steel. A metal kettle usually lasts a lot longer than a glass or ceramic one and is not susceptible to chipping and cracking.

The handle should be designed for easy pouring and should be solidly attached to the rest of the kettle. Newer kettles may have handles that stay cool to the touch even as the water boils.

When buying a new tea kettle, we make sure the lid comes off easily and allows us to reach in and thoroughly clean the inside. We have seen many kettles with lids that are too small and so make cleaning difficult. There are even kettles with no removable lids at all. These kettles must be filled through the wide spout. We do not like to think of conditions inside these kettles after a few months' use, and we never buy them.

If you prefer an electric kettle, follow the same suggestions as above. The kettle should be easy to clean, built to fit your hand and to pour easily. The best electric kettles allow you to immerse them completely in water for cleaning. Be sure to dry these kettles thoroughly before using again.

Teapot

Once you have a tea kettle for boiling the water, you can then think about the teapot. This is the vessel you will use to brew tea or to hold the hot water when you brew each cup separately.

When it comes to teapots, there is a seemingly endless variety of sizes, shapes, colors, materials and designs. In doing the research for this book, we found glass pots, ceramic pots and metal pots. Each of these came in many colors and shapes. If you enjoy collecting, then you may find yourself with a different teapot for each occasion.

Of all the teapots we tried, we prefer a simple ceramic pot with a solid glaze. Our all-time favorite is a white ceramic one-quart pot. It is easy to clean, pours well, and has a well-designed handle. The lid fits snugly and has a small hole in it to release steam. This prevents the hot water or tea from gushing out the spout when you put on the lid. On the outer edge of the lid there is a small tongue that fits under the rim of the teapot. This prevents the lid from falling off as you pour, a useful feature.

Our white teapot has a traditional squat shape. There is no mistaking it for anything but a teapot. We have also seen all sorts of whimsical designs for teapots, from gingerbread houses to various animals. No matter what you choose, look for a pot that is easy to clean, has a good pour, and fits your hand. It may be that you will use your everyday teapot when you do readings, or you may prefer a special pot or pots reserved just for tea leaf readings.

Our favorite tea pot: "Bird of Paradise" from France

We have also tried silver teapots. These are serviceable, and certainly present an elegant appearance. We found that silver teapots require a lot of maintenance, both in cleaning and polishing. If this is the sort of thing you enjoy, by all means use a silver pot. For our purposes, we prefer low maintenance equipment. We also found that a silver pot seems to add a slight off-flavor to the tea.

No matter your choice, it is important to keep the inside of the pot clean. The tannins in tea can build up on the inner surfaces of a teapot, especially if the pot has an odd shape with hidden corners. After a bit, this tannin build-up will affect the flavor of the tea. A sure-fire method for removing this build-up was passed down to us by family members. We put a bit of white vinegar in the teapot, add several tablespoons of baking soda, and pour in just-boiled water. The resulting chemical reaction will scour the pot clean with no further effort on your part.

When you are finished your reading, be sure to wash out the teapot and dry it thoroughly—generally sound advice for so many things in the kitchen. If your pot is valuable, be sure to put it away somewhere it will not be jostled or knocked over.

Some teapots come fitted with removable filters that fit inside and hold the tea. These contraptions are usually mesh filters in a plastic frame these days, but we have one ceramic teapot from France with a ceramic filter.

Hot Water Pot

If you choose to brew your tea in a pot rather than in individual cups, you may want to consider a separate pot for freshly boiled water. This way, you can mix the brewed tea and the hot water and produce a cup of tea of the desired strength.

One-and-a-half cup pot with one of our favorite reading cups.
This one-person set up allows for individual preferences in teas.

Having two pots in your tea service may seem a bit formal, but it does make a nice impression when you are doing a reading. Your guests will feel special when they see that you have taken the trouble to think of their varying preferences.

The hot water pot could be the same design as your teapot, or you could choose to have two different pots. This is a point where you can be creative. There are complete tea sets on the market where all the pieces share the same design, but you do not have to do it this way.

For our own readings, we chose two identical deep blue ceramic pots, one for the strong tea and one for the hot water. We found that having two of the same pots simplifies things for us, and we never have to worry about which pot to use for what.

Infuser

Some people prefer to spoon the tea leaves directly into the brewing pot and allow them to settle to the bottom as they steep in the boiling hot water. If they do this, then they will often stir the pot just before pouring so that each person has a complement of tea leaves in each individual cup. After all, it is hard to read the leaves if they are all in the pot!

Once the tea is poured in this fashion, the drinkers must allow the leaves to settle once again in each cup. And they have to sip gently so as not to disturb the leaves at the bottom of the cup.

Other people will brew each cup separately, spooning a measure of tea into a cup and then adding the hot water from a pot. In this way, each person has his or her own tea leaves. People who use this method seem to feel that it will provide a more personal reading. It is a nice theory, and if you are attracted to this method, then by all means use it. We remain unconvinced, thinking that what matters ultimately is the residue of tea leaves when the cup is drained and turned over.

In our practice, we use an infuser to hold the leaves in the brewing pot. We slowly pour the boiling water over these leaves, and we leave the infuser in the pot while the steeping takes place. We remove the infuser and the leaves when we judge the tea is at proper strength. We usually set the infuser and the leaves on a separate flat plate next to the teapot.

Two infusers with some Gunpowder tea: a mesh ball infuser (left);
a plastic and mesh insertable infuser (right); the larger infuser will
hold whole-leaf tea as well

When we have all enjoyed our tea, we add about a quarter of a cup of new tea from the pot and spoon some leaves from the infuser on the plate into each cup. These will be the leaves we read.

We use an infuser because we find that it allows us to brew the tea to the strength we prefer, prevents the tea leaves from adding too much bitterness to the brew and from clouding the contents of the cups. Since we are so keen on infusers, you might wonder if we have a preference. We do: ceramic infusers.

Infusers come in various sizes and substances. Of all that we have used, we prefer a two-inch across ceramic ball attached to a stainless chain-and-hook. The ball unscrews and we can spoon the tea into the bottom half. The ceramic is easy to keep clean and imparts no flavor to the tea or the water. The empty upper half of the infuser allows the tea leaves to expand as they steep.

We also have the porcelain teapot from France we mentioned earlier. This teapot is intended for brewing whole-leaf teas. The infuser, of the same design and substance as the pot (see photo p. 66), is long and has rather sizeable holes in it. It can be removed when the tea is strong enough. In this case, we wait until the tea leaves have cooled a bit—enjoying our tea in the meantime—and then chop the leaves before putting them into the individual cups.

We confess that it was another tea-reader who assured us it was permissible to chop up the leaves. Before that, we had always used the standard small pieces of tea leaves one finds on sale at most stores.

Other kinds of infusers we have used are: metal mesh balls of varying diameters, a stainless perforated metal ball, and a metal spoon infuser for individual cups. The metal infusers perform their function just as well as the ceramic ones, are readily available, and are inexpensive.

Of course, you might just decide to skip the entire infuser issue and use tea bags. This is also perfectly acceptable. You can either open the bags and pour the tea into the pot when you are ready to do a reading, or you can have the participants tear open their own bags and let the leaves fall into their cups.

Tea Caddy

When it comes to brewing tea, hot is best. There are few pleasures that turn so quickly awry than hot tea gone cold. To help keep your tea hot, tea caddies were invented. At its simplest, a tea caddie is a thick cloth folded up and used to cover the pot. The insulating layers of cloth hold in the heat.

Of course, humans being what they are, actual single-purpose tea caddies exist in abundance. Some of these fit snugly over the pot from the top, and others sit on the table and are drawn up over the pot. In either case, they act as insulators and keep your tea hot.

Tea caddies come in a great variety of colors and patterns. Choose something that suits you, and that harmonizes with the rest of your tea set. Remember that a tea caddie is not high-power insulation. Under a tea caddie the water in a pot will remain warmer than without one, but not for hours, or even much more than twenty minutes in our experience.

Tea Cups

If you want to do a tea leaf reading, even Styrofoam cups will do in a pinch, but some of that special feeling will be missing. The teacup is central to a reading. It should be well-shaped, aesthetically pleasing, and a pleasure to hold. This does not have to mean expensive. There are very nice everyday stoneware cups on the market that fit each of the above criteria and cost under three dollars each.

On the whole, we have found that wide and shallow tea cups work best for tea leaf readings: the leaves have more inner surface of the cup on which to form their designs. A wide shallow cup is also easier to "read" because the surface allows the leaves to remain in place. A deeper cup often causes the leaves to slip to the bottom

If you have everyday teacups that you like, then go right ahead and do your readings with them. It helps if the cup is white, cream, or light colored. This makes it easier to discern the distribution of the leaves inside. A dark cup may obscure the exact shapes the leaves take.

Of course, if you intend to do readings regularly, or if you want your readings to have a special air to them, you might want to think about having a set of bone china cups. Keep these for readings only; this will enhance your presentation and signal a truly special event. There are many kinds of bone china or porcelain cups with beautiful designs on the outside and a simple white interior. These are excellent choices for tea leaf readings.

If you want something really special, there are high quality porcelain cup-and-saucer sets sold individually. Each cup and saucer has a different, but harmonizing, design from the others in the series. This helps to emphasize the individuality of each person having his or her tea leaves read, and makes for a distinctive event.

Some of the tasseomancers we consulted prefer to use two cups for each person. One cup is for drinking the tea, and the other cup is for the reading. This is especially useful if the person having a reading done insists on having milk or cream in the tea. The second cup can be kept dairy-free so as not to obscure the leaves.

In this case, the tasseomancer pours a full cup for drinking, then a quarter-cup containing leaves in the second cup. The person having the leaves read drinks the tea in the first cup and allows the leaves in the second cup to settle. Most readers prefer to use just one cup per person. In either case, it is important to use attractive cups and saucers.

Saucers

We mentioned saucers several times above, and it is important to note that these are not just for looks. When the drinker has finished most of the tea in the cup, the leaves are allowed to settle, and then the cup is turned upside down onto the saucer. The cup is then righted, and the leaves are examined. A good, solid saucer with a defined rim is important for holding the remaining bit of tea and the excess leaves.

Our friend Renée could blithely do a reading from a Styrofoam cup and dump the excess liquid and leaves onto a small pile of paper napkins, but guests in your home may be dismayed at similar tactics. Presentation is an important facet of tasseomancy, so you will want to have things as nice as possible.

Spoons

Once again, our friend Renée set our preferences for nice spoons on edge when she insisted that plastic fast food spoons would serve just as well. We admit that the kind of spoon really does not matter much to the tea and the leaves, and will probably have no adverse effect on the reading. Nevertheless, we maintain that, for the sense of theatre so essential to a reading, silver spoons and such definitely add to the ambience.

Let us assume that you will choose to eschew plastic utensils at your readings. This leaves either stainless or silver. The advantages of stainless spoons and other tea utensils are many: lower initial cost, easier upkeep, and so on. And there are enough good looking stainless sets that you will find a wide choice of style and heft. Just find something that pleases you, and that seems to be practical for heavy use. Oddly enough, the simpler the design, the more scratches and wear will show, so consider the more ornate of stainless sets.

While silver requires constant attention and polishing, and has a higher initial cost, there is an indisputable something about a silver service that bespeaks the seriousness of purpose when you do a tea leaf reading. If you do not wish to invest in a complete silver set, perhaps just a few spoons for your readings will suffice.

Whether stainless or silver, a tea scoop is an excellent find. This scoop is just the right size to measure out enough tea for a cup, and several measures for a pot. If you have trouble finding a tea scoop, check the Internet sites in the appendix.

Tea Tray

Now that you have assembled your tea kettle, pot, cups and so on, there arises the question of how to transport the tea service to the table. We are firm believers in *presentation*, in seating our guests and then bringing in the service. To do this, we depend on several heavy silver trays. Of course, if you prefer, you can simply set everything out on the table before your guests arrive, and then bring in the tea and hot water when everyone is seated.

As long as you promise not to tell, we can reveal to you that we found our wonderful silver trays at a local flea market. Apparently, their previous owners had gotten tired of the constant need to polish the ornate trays, and had simply put them to the curb in frustration. At least, that is what we like to think. We cannot imagine anyone deliberately parting with these trays for any other reason.

In between tea leaf readings, we keep the trays tightly wrapped in plastic wrap. This prevents the worst of tarnishing, and all we have to do is give the trays a quick wipe before using.

When we are not at our fanciest, we have other trays that we use to transport the tea service: bamboo trays, a wood-and-ceramic set, and even, we admit it, several all-purpose plastic trays.

This completes our list of the items that go into a good tea service. You might also want to consider appropriate tablecloths, candles and napkins. The essential idea is to create a feeling of distinction, of something out of the ordinary. This feeling will help to set the stage for the reading, and your guests will be more receptive to your revelations.

In the next chapter we will discuss getting yourself into the right frame of mind to do a reading. How do you transform yourself from the workaday you into a powerful tasseomancer? Read on!

Tea Time!
hands-on adventures

1. What kind of equipment appeals to you? Classic British china? Asian styles? Modern or Retro American? Make a wish list of the items you would like to have among your tasseomancy tools.

2. Look around you at home. Without buying anything, can you get started in tasseomancy? Do you have everything you will need? Can you make do with some of the supplies?

3. Here is a suggestion: browse around on the Internet, in catalogs, in stores. Find the equipment you think will be perfect for your tea leaf readings. Keep a running tab of the cost. Compare prices.

4. What do you think about keeping a special, separate set of equipment for tea leaf reading? What might the benefits be? How can such a practice help you focus on the special nature of tasseomancy?

5. It's time to get your friends involved! Why not plan a time when everyone will bring an assortment of teacups? That way you will be able to try a variety of cups to see which are suitable for tasseomancy, and which are not. Try to keep track of the reasons for your judgements.

Part Two

The Art of
Tea Leaf Reading

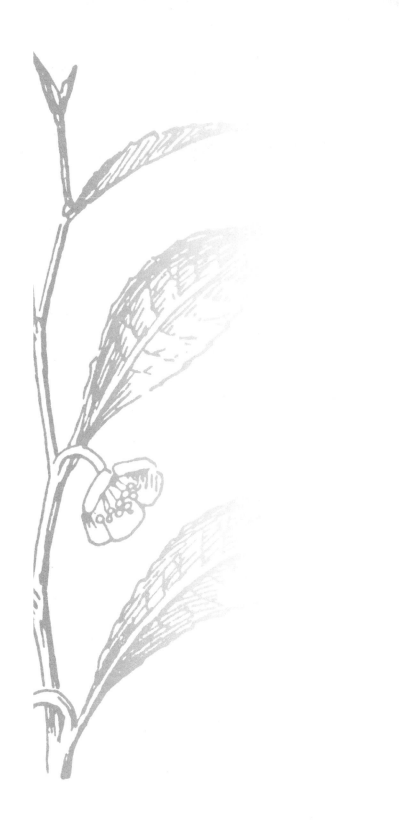

Chapter Six

Getting Into
The Mindset

A   nna, our grandmother and great-grandmother, was celebrated within
    her social circle for reading tea leaves. Often she would conduct a
    reading one-on-one with a seeker, but she especially loved setting up
her parlor for a tea reading party. Over the years she gained a reputation
not only as a reader, but also for making readings and observations which
were by and large relevant and accurate. She had a special system for deci-
phering the shapes that would appear in the tea leaves. Family stories of
Anna suggest that she learned the skill from her own mother and grandmother, and family lore also reveals that Anna developed a system of reading tea leaves entirely on her own. Either way, tea held a special magic for
her and for the people who came to her with questions.

Not everyone will feel the need to delve as deeply into tasseomancy as
Anna did, but all the same there is applicable wisdom in her methods. At
the heart of it all, she regarded her readings as something extraordinary. Her
preparation for a tea leaf reading often was almost as involved as the reading itself. She maintained a preparation room, something that modern people might call a meditation chamber, as well as a room for readings that
could accommodate one to a dozen. Different questions required different
kinds of tea in Anna's mind.

For a love or relationship question, Anna would use green tea. For
money and financial questions, she preferred to use Assam. She had a collection of teacups to suit every mood and need. In short, Anna regarded
reading tea leaves as a ritual, and, as with any ritual, tasseomancy required
preparation.

The goal of this chapter is to teach you different mental and spiritual
preparation techniques for performing your own tea leaf readings. After all,
the essential tool for tasseomancy is your mind. Without the ability to see
symbols and signs and make the connections to events, you will only be
staring down into a mass of soggy tea leaves. For the leaves to have any
meaning, your mind must be clear and able to interpret ambiguous shapes
and draw meaningful information from them.

Chances are good that you do not live the life of leisure enjoyed by
Victorian ladies of the parlor. You probably also do not have quite so much
time to devote to tea leaf reading as Anna did. Our modern lifestyle tends

not to allow a great deal of time for quiet reflection and thought. However, in order to read tea leaves successfully, you will need to make some time in your schedule. You will need to relax both your mind and your nerves. In this way will you become open and receptive to messages revealed in the leaves.

Fortunately, attaining the proper mindset is both simple and practical, if you know how. The mind of today is occupied by so many things—our families, our jobs, our obligations—that achieving this necessary state of mental relaxation may at first seem impossible. Of course it is possible, but training your mind to calm down at will takes some effort. We will take you through some practices to prepare your mind for the art of tasseomancy.

Your first step is to establish a place and time for your preparation and reading. Anna may have had two separate rooms for her practice, but this is not necessary. More than likely you will find your place in your own home. In case you do not, there is always the possibility of taking your tea on the road in a thermos. Since you are reading for your own tranquillity, find a quiet and private place where you can conduct your reading undisturbed. Reading for one or two other people may be done in the same place. However, if you are planning on holding a tea leaf reading party, you might want to spend more time grounding and centering your mind before joining the group. The most important element is that you are fully comfortable. The place you have chosen for your preparation should resonate with your being and allow you to feel absolutely confident.

Once you are physically comfortable, you need to bring comfort to your mind. The following paradigm can help you understand the internal process by which your mind will be able to interpret tea leaves. This way of imagining the mind is in terms of the *Higher Self* and the *Lower Self.* These expressions do not refer to physical states of being, but rather to mental phases.

Your Lower Self is the you that you are in normal, everyday life. The Lower Self is the you that interacts with other people and with the world. Think of it as your conscious self, that part of you that is aware of everything going on around you right at this moment. It is the Lower Self that will deliver the reading to yourself or to the person for whom you are doing the reading.

The Higher Self is just as present as the Lower Self, but not in the same immediate and tangible way. Your Higher Self is your thinking self, your dreaming self, and the seat of your imagination. This is the part of yourself that is most open to suggestions, new perceptions, and abstractions such as images in damp tea leaves.

In order to be a successful tasseomancer, you need the Lower Self and the Higher to communicate. Essentially, the Lower Self makes the initial reading of the patterns of the leaves. It notices the placement and shapes. These impressions are relayed to the Higher Self, which in turn translates these patterns into meaningful symbols. The connection between the two Selves needs to be open, with a free flow of images and patterns. You can easily promote communication between the Selves through the following activities.

One excellent technique that you can practice anywhere is meditative breathing. This means you will make yourself aware of every breath you draw. You will feel the rush of air entering your body and filling your lungs. Then you will experience the release as you exhale. Be mindful of each breath you take. As you focus on your breathing, your immediate attachment to the outside world will fall away until your mind is relaxed and ready to read.

On a more advanced level, the time between breathing in and breathing out becomes more important. Become aware of that brief pause when you have filled your lungs but have not yet begun to exhale. Perhaps you will decide to extend the pause a bit in order to have time to explore your perceptions. Great depth is there, but this is something that comes on its own.

In another technique, you might also take yourself on a dream voyage while you are awake. Called visualization, this is the practice of summoning imagery into your mind. Bring this imagery to a point of clarity where it seems like reality for you. Visualization takes some effort but the results can transport you into entirely new surroundings. Imagine yourself standing on a beach with sand like sugar, boating on a roaring river in a rain forest valley, or even floating through space in the company of stars. If you can visualize it, you can use it to prepare your mind. Through visualization, you can turn the abstract into a kind of reality.

Another enjoyable way to get yourself into the proper mindset for tasseomancy is a pre-reading bath. A tub full of warm water is an excellent place to collect your thoughts. You can relax both your mind and your body. To enhance the ambience, you might want to add fragrant oil to the bath water. If you have only a shower, call it a sauna and have a good time relaxing under the warm stream, luxuriating in the steam and the sound of the water..

As might be expected, a great way to relax before a reading is by drinking a cup of hot tea. We recommend grounding and centering with some green tea. Teas made from herbs are gently powerful and can be especially effective. Here are our suggestions. Be advised that these recommendations come from our own experiences in herbalism. We are not medical doctors. Please check with your physician before using these or any herbs.

Mint—Any of the mint teas deliver a wonderful flavor along with a soothing calm.

Basil—With a slight taste of licorice, basil tea relaxes body and mind.

Linden—The subtle flavor of linden makes a tea that is wonderful for the nerves.

Anise—A pronounced flavor makes anise tea a favorite among herbalists.

Bay—The leaves of the bay laurel tree have been favored by seers since the days of ancient Greece.

Chamomile—These delicate flowers make a subtle tea.

Catnip—Also called catmint, this leaf herb is best used in small amounts.

Dandelion Root—Many people find that this tea tastes pleasantly similar to coffee.

Fennel—Use the fennel seed to make this tea.

Lavender—The tea is made from the small flowers and also has a slight licorice flavor.

Rose—This beautiful flower makes a surprisingly tasty tea.

Yarrow—Appropriately enough, yarrow tea is a favorite among diviners.

The standard rule of thumb is one tablespoon of ground herb to one cup of boiling water. You may decide whether less or more of the herb suits you. Another possibility is mixing these herbs to make new brews to suit your palate. Pour the water over the herb mixture and let it steep for at least fifteen minutes.

In all reality, the act of brewing tea, whether it be for yourself or for the reading, is itself a ritual that can put your mind at ease. Everything from the teapot to the cups to the tea leaves themselves is a psychological cue. If you plan to make tea leaf readings on a regular basis, consider the rite of preparation as a means of focusing your mind.

Finally, we should look at some verbal practice. By this we mean actual practiced phrases that you will say out loud in order to alert your mind to the coming reading. Sit on the floor or on the ground in a quiet area. If you want, add to the mood with your favorite incense and music. Light a few candles. Begin with some meditative breathing as described earlier. Then use a favorite chant or mantra to bring your mind into readiness. We have included the following examples for your immediate use.

Chants

I

I gaze upon these leaves of tea
So that Fate may be clear to me.
Close to me or far away,
Tell me where I am today.
What is to come, what is to be,
Open my mind and leave it free.
Show me these signs of which I have heard
A tree, a mountain, a flower, a bird.
The tea and I, we speak the same.
Tell me the secrets as you would speak my name.

II

Open my mind to the signs.
This cup is my stage, these leaves are my actors.
Drop away from the stress of this world.
Floating above far into the possible,
Past, present, future in my hands,
The cycle continues, and I am a part.
Prepare my thoughts for this revelation,
Wide to possibility and free to chance.
Suggestion, find me to interpret the leaves.
May I use this knowledge with wisdom.

III

The cup resembles the bowl of the sky,
And the leaves become the stars.
Where in the cup do the leaves fall?
How do the stars make constellations?
Look for possibilities as wide as the skies.
Ground, and center, and focus, and explore.
Expand, contract, empower your imagination.
What the leaves say will depend on what you see.
Have no limits, no doubts, no hesitation.
The power of knowing is in your hands.

Mantras

1. The tea tells all.
2. Tea speaks a wisdom unknown to all else.
3. When in doubt, read the tea.
4. By leaves and cup, be one with the ancients.
5. Tea knows.
6. What a wondrous world we could make if we consult the leaves!
7. The person who asks the leaves seeks wisdom.
8. Seeing what you wish in the leaves only means it is possible.
9. Warm in the body, inspiration in the mind.

In the end, how you ease yourself into tea reading is up to you. That you give your mind a little training is essential.

Tea Time!
hands-on adventures

1. Think about the mystic meaning in the leaves. The leaves themselves are passing on information to you. Now think about approaching tasseomancy from the viewpoint of psychology. The tea leaves form shapes that you subconsciously interpret according to your own personality and experiences. Which of these two approaches works best for you? Do you think both interpretations might be two sides of the same coin?

2. Think about creating the best ambience for a tea leaf reading. What will you do? How can you arrange the area where you will do the reading so that your guests get into the proper mood? Will music help? How about lighting?

3. What external influences might affect your tea leaf reading? Think of some positive influences as well!

4. Is there a certain time of day you feel will be better for tasseomancy? Do you think you might like to do noontime readings? How about a certain day or days? You are the tasseomancer, so you get to choose your time and place.

5. Why not throw a party? Start to think about how you would hold a tea leaf reading session for a group of friends and loved ones. How could you create your own reading parlor? Where would you do your readings?

Chapter Seven

The Compass
and the Cup

In tasseomancy we use the word *querent* to refer to the person for whom the tea leaf reading is being done. We thought it might be interesting to talk a bit about the origins of this word before we go on with our discussion.

Querent belongs in the family of words that includes *query, inquire* and even question. The base on which these words are formed is the Latin verb *quaerere*, "to seek, make an inquiry, to ask for." The present participle— *quaerens/quaerentis*," (one who is) seeking, asking"—gives us querent in English. In compounds, the Latin verb has the form *-quirere*, as in *inquirere*, "to inquire." And, as happens frequently in Latin, the *r* can become an *s*: *quaestio/quaestionis*, "a question." So, if the tasseomancer or reader is the one interpreting the leaves, the querent is the person for whom the reader is gazing into the cup.

Tea leaf readings depend upon two elements: where the leaves settle in the cup and what patterns they reveal to the reader. Considering the location of the leaves is much like reading a map. Where leaves collect in the upturned bowl of the tea cup provides an integral point of reference to the reading.

Tasseomancy is by no means an exact science. However, a kind of mystic cartography is an essential aspect of a reading. Without considering leaf symbols in combination with given "coordinates" in the cup, a reading may still be accurate but will have no sense of timing or orientation.

We should begin with the handle. This represents you on the map of the cup. The handle is your point of reference. If you are doing a reading for yourself, you will keep the handle turned towards you. By doing this, you will see how the leaves have collected in direct relation to you. When you do a reading for someone else—the querent, as we have explained— keep the handle turned toward that person and consider the message of the leaves from that person's perspective.

Imagine the cup evenly split down the middle into a left and a right hemisphere. This maps the past, the present, and the future of your life. Symbols you see in the left hemisphere indicate events and influences moving into your life, while those in the right hemisphere show what is departing from your life. What you see close to the middle would be depicting what is occurring in your life at the moment.

Naturally you would want to know how far off in the future or how soon you are going to meet that new sweetheart or have to get your roof fixed. The measure in the tea cup for this is the bottom up to the rim. The closer to the bottom you see an occurrence, the farther off in the future it is. However if your leaves are gathered near the rim, you may find the result of your reading standing right behind you.

You can also use the relative position of the handle in making a reading. If the handle is you, then anything appearing away from the handle is less likely to affect you. Perhaps it is a glimpse of something important to a friend or a loved one.

If you are reading the leaves for someone else, the same principles apply, but now the references will be to that other person's life and activities.

Any symbols that you spot on the rim of the cup indicate events and conditions of extreme importance to querent. When we say importance, we mean of potentially life-changing significance. In contrast, symbols along the sides of the cup represent important events, but nothing life-changing. What you see at the bottom of the cup suggests what may occur, but is subject to change. Of course, in reality any glimpse of the future is only a look at what might be. You are writing your own future all of the time, so never get terrified if your reading is something less optimistic than you would like. It is a good idea to remind the querent of this as you proceed with the reading.

To clarify this idea that the future remains alterable until it becomes the present, we can use an example from everyday life, imagine a vending machine with twenty-five different snacks in it. Each snack is labeled *A-1*, *B-1*, etc. At the moment you put money into the machine, *every snack is a possibility*. Now, as soon as you push the button *C*, all the snacks with other letters have been ruled out. And once you follow the *C* with the number *4*, only one snack is now possible, *C-4*. In the same way, possibilities for the future are many, and it is only in making choices between the present and the future that specific possibilities become more—or less—probable. Your reading will reveal what *may yet be*, not what *will surely be*. It is important to keep this in mind.

Here is an example of the geography within the cup using the glossary of symbols in Chapter Eight. The leaves are randomly spread around the cup. You clearly see an acorn on the rim and read that querent will experience financial success in the near future. Maybe the symbols seem to form a spiral. You see a face, a fountain, and a coin. Your interpretation is that the querent will soon have a change in friendships that will bring great happiness and prosperity.

There are still other straightforward patterns to consider in your readings. Symbols that lie in straight lines may be indicating events that will almost certainly occur in the future. A curved or a wavy line is a marker of change. If in your reading you come across a symbol that you find absolutely clear and unambiguous, it could refer to an event that is likely to occur. On the other hand, if you see a symbol that requires careful interpretation and imagination, this probably refers to an event that is less likely to occur. When looking into the cup, check for obvious patterns such as numerals, lines, shapes, and letters. Use these symbols first.

Even with these rules and suggestions, remember that your greatest asset is your own intuition. Let it speak. Listen to it. Your intuition is capable of seeing much more in a tea leaf reading than your eyes, no matter how adept a reader you may be.

Tea Time!
hands-on adventures

1. You have read about the coordinates and the relative positions of the tea leaves in the cup. Why not make a diagram for yourself of the inside of a cup and the meaning of the various positions in terms of time and importance. Don't forget to include the *handle* of the teacup as your starting point. If you are artistic, this diagram could turn into a wonderful poster!

2. Before you begin to do readings for others, how about doing several for yourself? This way, you will not be pressured to "see" what is not there, and you will gain experience in interpreting what you see.

3. Here's another way to progress: have a friend do some readings for you. See if you agree with what the friend finds in the cup. *Hint:* don't make a big fuss if your friend seems totally off-target. It might be better if you didn't make any negative comments.

4. Let's imagine that the reader has told you, "There will be a change in where you live. You will be moving to a new location." What practical steps could you take to increase the probability of this happening? How could you decrease the probability of this being the correct reading?

5. *Intuition* derives from the Latin verb intueri, "to look inward or upon." How would you rate your intuition? Do you "get" things? How do you think intuition will help you in tasseomancy?

Chapter Eight

The Meaning
in the Leaves

Befffore we give you a list of the shapes you may find in the leaves, we want to tell you about a reading we went to while researching this book. We headed west from our home, out into the countryside. After seventy minutes on the road, we reached the outskirts of Reading, Pennsylvania. This Reading is pronounced "redding." The small city of Reading was once famous for its outlet shops and besieged by shopping-crazed tourists all year round. Now the place has returned to its backwater days and things were a lot quieter.

Following the e-mailed instructions, we pulled into the large parking lot surrounding the Berks County Restaurant (for personal reasons, our contact did not want us to use the actual name of the restaurant). Cars—mostly SUVs, vans, and pickups—crowded the part of the lot nearest the entrance. Over on the side were ten or twelve tractor-trailer rigs. This was obviously a popular spot, more of an overgrown diner than a fancy restaurant.

Inside, we asked to sit in the dining room as our contact, Netta, had told us. We came in during the busiest part of the dinner rush, so we read through the menu quickly. At the bottom of the last page was the notice we had been looking for: "Tuesday, Wednesday and Thursday, free tea leaf readings with your after-dinner tea from 5:30 until 7:30. Find your future in a cup of our special tea."

Netta was the reader. She had contacted us when she heard about this book. Netta thought it would be good for us to see a hard-working reader in an everyday location. "Nothing fancy," she had written, "just plain folks who enjoy the occasional reading. And nothing serious: I give general information about the near future."

We had dinner—great prices, good food—then lingered over dessert. As we looked around, we noticed a woman who had to be Netta moving quietly from table to table. Netta looked to be in her mid-forties. She was dressed in a blue party gown with matching shoes and a big bow in her light brown hair. She had lots of gold jewelry: rings, bracelets, two necklaces. Netta also had bright red lipstick and an infectious smile. As we watched, Netta spent about five minutes with each client.

Our waitress came by. As she gathered up the dessert dishes, she asked, "Would you folks like some of our special tea and a reading? Miss Netta there is pretty good."

"What's special about the tea?" I asked.

"It's loose tea," the waitress answered, "not the kind in tea bags. And we use plain white cups and saucers. The tea leaf reading is free with the tea."

Of course we ordered two special teas. The waitress brought two cups and a small teapot with loose tea brewing in a mesh infuser.

"Be sure to leave about a quarter-inch of tea in your cups," the waitress said as she left for another table.

We sipped our tea and watched Netta continue to work the room. After about twenty-five minutes, it was our turn. Netta came over smiling.

"Hi, Netta!" I said. "It's us, the people doing the tea book."

Netta shook our hands. "It sure is nice to meet you folks. I'm glad you could make it out here." She sat down at our table.

"You look busy," my partner stated. "Is it always like this?"

"Oh, sure! I think Thursdays are our busiest nights for readings. I get here around five, gather my thoughts in the back room, and start making my rounds right at half-past. I usually work straight through until seven-thirty. Most Thursdays, I'm here until going on eight."

"I had no idea there was such interest in tea leaf reading," I said.

"Well, we're right off the Interstate, so there's a lot of travelers that stop here. And I get a good bit of repeat business from local folk as well. Tea leaf readings are not thought of as anything exotic around here, just a way to have some fun after dinner."

As she spoke, Netta took a spoon and scooped some tea leaves out of the infuser. She put a spoonful of leaves in each cup.

"Okay, now take your spoon and stir the leaves. As you do so, think of some question you would like answered, something general."

We did as Netta requested. Then we sat for a moment while the leaves settled in the cups. As tradition dictated, Netta asked us to turn our cups upside down on the saucers, then turn them rightside up. She looked into my cup first.

"I like to get a general view of the leaves before I look for specific shapes," she explained as she turned the cup around on the saucer.

Netta then did two competent readings, hitting all the major points according to the distribution of the leaves. Of course, in this case, we were more interested in finding out about Netta herself. It was already five after seven, so we decided to wait and talk to her at the end of her readings.

"How did you learn to do tea leaf readings?" I asked as Netta came back and sat at our table.

"Oh, I learned from a friend. She picked up a book in Reading about ten years ago. She did some readings for me and I borrowed the book. It just seemed to come naturally to me."

"How did you get this job?" I asked.

"The owner wanted something to set his place off from the other eateries around here. Someone suggested tea leaf readings to him, he placed an ad in the local paper, I answered on a whim and here I am."

"What kind of arrangement to you have here?" my partner asked.

"I come in three nights a week and work two hours. I'm usually home by eight, except on Thursdays."

"Is this your main form of employment?" I inquired.

"Goodness, no!" Netta answered laughing. "I have a day job in Reading. I do this mostly for fun. I make a little extra money, but nothing spectacular. I get paid per hour and pick up tips for my services. Because I'm so dependable, the owner lets my husband Nick eat here the three nights I work."

"How are the clients? Do they believe in tasseomancy?" I continued, jotting down Netta's responses in my notebook.

"Tasseomancy! That sure is a fancy word for what I do, isn't it? I guess we could charge more if we used tasseomancy instead of tea leaf reading! But I think folks around here just like the personal attention I give to their lives. As I said, I give general readings, we chat a bit and my clients are satisfied."

"Do you do any other kind of readings?" my partner asked. "Tarot? Crystal gazing?"

"No, no," Netta answered, clearly troubled by the idea. "That's all magic stuff, the way I see it. I stick to plain old tea leaves. That Tarot stuff is too weird for me!"

We thanked Netta for her tip about the restaurant and for her time. She shook our hands once again and headed back into the kitchen to get her coat. As we were paying at the counter, we saw her leave with Nick, her husband. We thought again how interesting it was that tea leaf reading was an accepted activity in this region, and how an ordinary woman could have a regular job providing information about patrons' futures.

We don't know exactly *which* book on tea leaf reading Netta's friend loaned her, but we have a feeling the meanings given to various shapes were pretty much like the ones we have found elsewhere. To help you get a better feel for the meanings in the shapes, we compiled the following glossary of symbols from many sources. To the handwritten notes in our own family records we have been able to add suggestions from other tasseomancers, as well as a few from books featuring tasseomancy. Of course there is no master list, and there is no one absolute way to read the leaves. Since identifying symbolism in wet leaves is not immediately easy and does take some time to master, we wanted to give you a strong start. You may very well write your own glossary of symbolic meaning in the future.

Some of the leaf matter might gather in clumps that form clearly distinct shapes. Begin your reading by examining the simplest and most obvious symbols first. For example, letters may suggest the names of friends and loved ones. A number could indicate a span of time, as in the number 3 for three years or three months.

Often the leaves will seem to form random shapes on the inner surface of the cup. This is where your intuition and experience will come to your aid. Below we have provided a list of symbols and a general reading for each one.

ACORN	– the promise of financial success
AIRCRAFT	– generally indicates travel by air
AMBULANCE	– a bad omen of sickness
ANCHOR	– stagnation
ANGEL	– the arrival of happy news
ANTS	– overcoming impending troubles
APPLE	– great prosperity and achievement
ARROW	– strong protection, or a direction
AUTOMOBILE	– generally lucky, usually indicates a journey·
AXE	– protection from evil
BABY	– new beginning, wish fulfillment
BALL	– good luck
BAT	– warning of intruders in the dark
BEAR	– strength and courage
BEAVER	– harbinger of an icy winter
BED	– sleepless nights to come
BELL	– good harvest, healing, soothing
BIRD	– can indicate good or bad luck depending on the kind of bird

BOARS/PIGS — seems to indicate either luck or evil
BOAT — friends will soon visit
BOOK — open: an answer is coming;
closed: a need for an answer
BOTTLE — potential for sickness
BREAD — expect a visitor
BRIDGE — navigate your path carefully
BROOM — the coming of something new
BUBBLES — financial good fortune
BUCKET — physical work
BULL — an argument with friends
BUTTERFLY — expect happiness

Middle, left to right: bridge, acorn, bird.

CANDLE — light in a dark situation
CAT — fortune in endeavors involving wit and cunning
CHILD — an innovative idea
COIN - prosperity
COYOTE — be mindful of your wits

COW	– abundance
CROSS	– sacrifice, reward after suffering
DAISY	– the arrival of a new love
DOG	– bad luck (no offense to dog lovers)
DOVE	– peace
DRUM	– change is coming
EGG	– broken: a setback; whole: success
ENVELOPE	– good news
EYE	– take caution
FACE	– changes will occur in a friendship
FINGER	– a warning
FLAG	– danger ahead
FOOT	– walking away from the past
FORK	– a decision needs to be made
FOUNTAIN	– abundant happiness
FISH	– peace in the home and in the community
FROG	– someone will entrust you with a secret
FRUIT	– bounty, hope
GARDEN	– a social event

Middle left: drum; *top center:* eye; *below "eye":* fish.

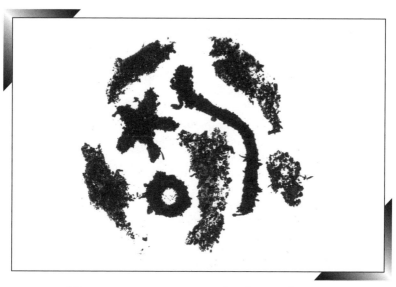

Lower middle: ring; *top center:* star; *right of "star" downward:* snake.

GLOBE	– plan to travel
GOAT	– wealth is attainable
GUN	– upsetting arguments with loved ones
HAND	– someone will offer assistance
HARP	– the bliss of romance
HAT	– an upcoming honor
HOUSE	– comfort, stability
ICEBERG	– lack of self-understanding
KANGAROO	– upcoming journey
KETTLE	– peace in the home
KITE	– wishes will come true
LADDER	– success in business
LEAF	– a new path in life
LOCK	– obstacles are everywhere
MASK	– the secret must be kept
MOUSE	– thievery
MUSHROOM	– a disturbance in the future
NET	– entrapment

OAK	– strength and health
OWL	– ambiguous fortune
OYSTER	– passionate love
PALM TREE	– thoughts of tropical paradises
QUESTION MARK	– questionable moral judgement
RABBIT	– bravery
RAT	– dishonesty
RING	– upcoming union
ROSE	– fame and popularity
SEASHELL	– good news
SHOE	– energy and productivity
SNAKE	– an enemy
SPIDER	– reward for work
STAR	– eternal hope
SWORD	– future arguments
TEAPOT	– friends
TOWER	– disappointment
TREE	– good health
TURTLE	– criticism is coming
UMBRELLA	– protection
VASE	– a secret admirer
VOLCANO	– emotional upset
WAGON	– adversity ahead
WATERFALL	– abundance
WHEEL	– advancement through great effort

Tea Time!
hands-on adventures

1. The glossary contains a list of symbols and their *suggested* meanings. You are entirely free to use and change the glossary as suits you. From your experience so far, are there additions you would like to make? Perhaps it would be a good idea to keep a notebook of your readings and the shapes you encounter. This will become your own personal *Tea Journal*, the essential companion for all tea leaf readers.

2. Looking back at the symbols and their meanings, do you find you are in general agreement with the interpretations? Do some of the meanings seem far removed from the symbol or shape?

3. Just for fun, why not "create" a reading? Jot down five symbols from the above list. Now, place those symbols at various places inside the cup. Remember to consider where they are relative to the handle, which is pointed at your querent. Interpret the symbols as if you were doing an actual reading.

4. When you look at the tea leaves in a cup, you may not be sure of exactly which shape you are seeing. Sometimes you will hesitate between two (or more!) possible symbols. Think about how you will handle this when you are doing a reading for a querent. What will you do if the querent thinks he or she sees a symbol different from the one you are talking about?

5. Tasseomancy is not like doing people's income tax: we try to avoid bad news and negative readings. Imagine that you find an arrangement of leaves in the cup that seem to indicate some negative things in the querent's future. How will you handle that? How can you be honest about what you see while at the same time avoiding a negative reading?

Chapter Nine

How to Read
the Leaves

Now it is time to put everything you have learned together and try an actual tea leaf reading. Before you go "live"—that is, before you start reading for other people—you may want to do a few test readings in order to get comfortable with the leaves. This means that you can take as much time as you need to make sense of the patterns in your cup. Keep this book with you as you venture into your first readings. By working on your own, you will be gaining on-the-job experience as a tasseomancer, an advantage that simply reading this book cannot give you.

Later in the chapter we will be presenting photographs of sample leaf patterns. We will point out what symbols and shapes we find and explain what part they play in an overall reading. But before we get to this visual presentation, we should talk about the actual method for reading tea leaves. In truth, this is the method passed onto us from Grandmother Anna, the family tasseomancer. But our research has borne out that Anna's method is either similar or identical to the common instructions for performing a reading, and as we are the most familiar with it, we will be using Anna's wisdom.

You are going to practice tasseomancy on yourself. Why not make it useful? Have a question or an issue (for instance, *what is your romantic future?*) firmly in your mind, something that you would like to have resolved through interpreting the leaves in your cup. This is essentially what you would ask another person for whom you might be doing a reading.

Place a kettle full of water on a lit stove burner. Put your dry tea leaves into a bowl while the water is coming to a boil, and stir the leaves with your fingers. Try to concentrate on your question or your issue. Understand that the nature of your query is coming into contact with the tea leaves this way. Your water will be ready just as it comes to a rolling boil. Place your tea leaves into the teapot you intend to use for tasseomancy and then pour in the water. Brew the tea with the leaves loose within the teapot.

After about five minutes, stir the tea in the pot to distribute the leaves and pour some of the tea into your reading cup. Let it cool. Perhaps this does not seem like a proper way to make tea. But you are not making a nice tea for drinking. You are making tasseomancy tea, and you should follow a different procedure.

Wait until the tea is almost at room temperature. Sip the liquid and concentrate on your specific question. If you cannot think of anything in particular, perhaps you will want to give yourself a general prediction. In that case clear your mind while sipping the tea instead of focusing on something in particular. Leave a tiny bit of liquid (about one-quarter of an inch) and most of the tea leaves in the bottom of the cup. Be careful! It is really easy to swallow the tea leaves.

Take the cup in your left hand. Swirl it around clockwise (to the right) three times. Cover the top of the cup with your right hand. Make sure to swirl the leaves completely up and around the sides and rim of the cup.

Use a saucer of a size commensurate with your cup. Take the cup, turn it upside down and put it on the saucer. When you pick the cup up again, you may have a mess on the saucer, but more importantly you will have leaves in various patterns in your cup. This is the material for your reading. Now is the time to use the skills explained in Chapters Six, Seven, and Eight to interpret the tea leaves. We understand from our own experiences that the first time you try to read the leaves can be both difficult and frustrating. Keeping this in mind, we will begin with some examples of tea leaf patterns you might see in a cup. At first, you will be reading a written description. By the end of this chapter, you will have moved on to actual photos of leaves in cups.

As you read the following examples of the arrangement of tea leaves, think how you would interpret the meaning in each cup. Then read the following section where we tell you what various experienced tasseomancers said. For this section and the one with the photos, as you discover the interpretations, please remember that what we are presenting is only one way a particular cup can be deciphered. You may see these arrangements and pictures and have a completely different sense of how the leaves should be read. That is fine. Our purpose is to give you a practice, with visual aids at the end, and if you can take that image and come up with a different interpretation, you are well on your way to being a skilled tasseomancer.

To begin, think of each arrangement of leaves like cards dealt at Bridge, or in Poker. The leaves are your "hand," and you will have to decide what to do, how to interpret them. Take your time, think about each situation.

You may find that you can visualize the leaf-patterns more easily if you draw a circle and sketch in the shapes in the positions we describe.

1. In the first cup, the leaves cluster mostly around the handle. You see something that looks like and automobile and another shape like a bottle in close proximity to the handle. In the left hemisphere of the cup, you see what looks to you like a drum. On the right side of the handle, there is something that appears to be a daisy.

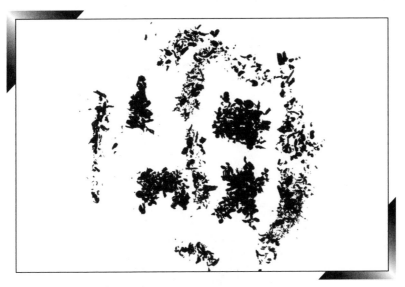

1. *Top left:* bottle; *bottom left:* auto; *center:* drum; *right:* daisy.

2. Much of the action in the second cup is near the brim. A large circle accompanies an axe and a bell in the right hemisphere.

3. In the third cup, you see symbols here and there, but they are concentrated near the bottom. You see something that looks like a kite and another shape that resembles a small house. The one large shape, considerably bigger than the other two shapes, resembles a mask.

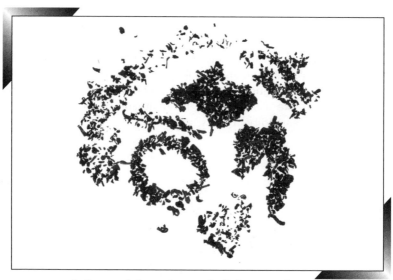

2. *Bottom left:* circle; *top:* bell; *lower right:* axe.

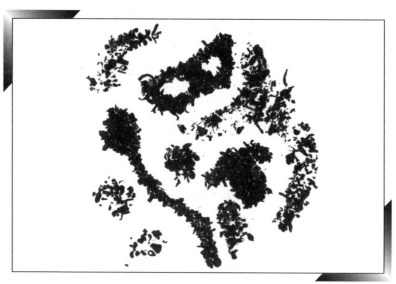

3. *Left, top to bottom:* kite; *top center:* mask; *bottom center:* small house.

4. *Top left:* oak leaf; *upper right:* two mushrooms.

5. *Top left:* iceberg; *top center:* question mark; *center right:* rat; *bottom center:* gun.

4. The fourth cup contains one predominant symbol: an oak leaf. The distinctive shape is clearly much larger than the other small forms. These other patterns in the leaves resemble small mushrooms. They are scattered all around the cup.

5. Finally, in the fifth cup, the left hemisphere presents a leaf-pattern that looks like a rat. There are also the shapes of an iceberg and a gun. Near the handle, the leaves have formed a kind of question mark. The right hemisphere of the cup is relatively empty.

Do you think your querents would enjoy your readings? Of course, once you figure out what the patterns *mean*, you can then work on dressing up your presentation with more dramatic language. Add a little mystery to your patter.

As we promised, here is a reading for each of the five situations we presented above. Let us remind you that, although we have hinted at the wide geographical area covered by our tea leaf readers, we have used initials to protect their privacy. This is what the various tasseomancers said:

1. *P. S.* in Kennewick, Washington, believes that the concentration of leaves near the handle of the cup indicates that the reading will have a strong influence on the querent. The automobile and the bottle are indicators of what may affect the querent either immediately or in the near future. While the automobile is a lucky symbol that often portends a journey, the bottle warns of a risk of falling ill. Together, these two shapes can be interpreted as a good upcoming trip on which the querent may become ill. The reader warns the querent to take the necessary precautions, such as traveling with appropriate medicines and telephone numbers. The drum in the left hemisphere of the cup indicates that a great change was on its way sometime in the recent past. Did it come to fruition? The querent may want to talk about this. Finally, the reader hopes that the querent is in the mood for a new love in the future. The daisy in the right hemisphere indicates that this is coming.

2. *K. B.* of Petersborough, Ontario, Canada, notices immediately that the leaves are mostly near the brim of the cup. The details of this reading will affect the querent very soon. All of the leaves also fall in the right hemi-

sphere, and this sets the reading up as a revelation of the future. On the whole, the reading contains a lot of good for the querent. The most significant symbol, the large circle, promises great prosperity. The axe foretells protection from evil, and the bell predicts healing.

3. *P. T.* of Charlemagne, Québec, Canada, sees the predominant feature of this reading as the large mask so clearly present in the leaves. Since the symbols of this reading are on the bottom of the cup, they represent concerns in the querent's distant future. The mask speaks of a secret that must be kept no matter what. The exact secret to be kept lies in the future. The kite is a more reassuring symbol: it means that wishes will come true. Finally, the house symbol suggests comfort and stability in the future.

4. *M. V.* of Baytown, Texas, first takes note of the large oak leaf present in the tea leaves. This obviously represents a predominant influence on the querent. The oak leaf symbolizes the arrival of steady strength and good health. The little mushrooms found throughout the rest of the leaves suggest a pattern of disturbances, but the stronger power of the oak leaf will overcome these problems.

5. *M. M.* of Havre de Grace, Maryland, tackles the fifth reading. He notices that the querent's past has not been full of kind experiences. The rat indicates dishonesty, the iceberg shows a lack of self-awareness and the gun represents upsetting arguments with loved ones. But the positions of these symbols show us that all these upsets are in the past. The question mark close to the handle suggests that the querent is on the brink of making a moral and ethical decision that will affect the future. The empty right side of the cup most likely signifies that future events will be contingent upon this particular decision.

Did you find that you agreed with our group of tasseomancers, or did you have a different take on reading the leaves? Remember, if it makes sense to you, and you have learned how to read the cup, then your reading is just as probable as anyone else's.

Tea Time!
hands-on adventures

For a change of pace, there is only one suggested activity for this chapter, rather than the several ideas you have seen in other chapters. Very simply, brew some tea, allow some leaves to remain in the bit of liquid at the bottom of the cup, overturn the cup and right it again. Now, *look into the leaves.* Quick! What are the first symbols you see? Where are they? In a notebook, jot down these initial impressions. Do not worry about interpreting the symbols just yet. The next step is to think of the symbols in terms of time: are these past, near future or distant future statements? Now think of their relevance to the querent: are they likely to be quite influential, only moderately active or barely noticeable? Once you have established these ideas, then you can consider the meanings of the symbols. Take the most prominent one or ones first. Work your way through to the lesser symbols. Do not attempt to read every tea leaf! Sometimes there are extraneous formations that really do not concern the tasseomancer.

Whew! That was a lot all at once. But you did it! That is the good news. Now for the rest: do it again. In fact, do it five, ten, sixteen times until you feel you are getting the hang of it. The more you practice, the better you will become.

Chapter Ten

Not Just for
Tea Drinkers

I climbed up the steps from the subway into the hubbub that is late after-noon around City Hall in Philadelphia. The *I* here is me, Emilie. My friend had just gotten out of class at a nearby university and was wait-ing for me at our favorite coffee house. Weaving through the crowd, I got my bearings and headed directly for Zando's.

"Sorry I'm late," I said. "I got caught up in writing my manuscript on tea leaf reading."

She rolled her eyes. "You're still on that fortune telling kick? Why don't you try reading the future in garbage?"

"Next book." I sat down and dropped my backpack onto the floor.

Sipping from a bottle of spring water, she regarded me evenly. "You're really serious."

I shrugged my shoulders. "It would be hard for me to deny. I've told you about Anna?"

She nodded. "Your great-grandmother, or something like that."

"Right. Anna took what today would be called a scientific approach to tea leaf reading. She recorded everything. When I got to read her notes, the whole practice suddenly made perfect sense to me."

"Okay, I'll pretend I'm open-minded. Convince me." She leaned towards me and in a conspiratorial whisper asked, "How does it work?"

"I'll do better than explain it. I'll show you." I turned to look at the menu. There wasn't much in the way of tea available, or at least nothing I felt competent to read. However, there were some perfect coffee options.

"Go order yourself a Turkish coffee."

"Coffee?" She arched her eyebrows. "I thought you read tea leaves."

"Reading coffee grounds uses the same principle. The point here is to show you how it's done."

"And why Turkish coffee? It's so strong! Tastes like boiled cigar butts if you ask me."

I laughed. "Be that as it may, Turkish coffee is served with the coffee grounds in the cup. Those grounds are what we're going to be reading."

Resigning herself to drinking cigars, she stretched her arms above her head. "All right, you're on. Watch my bag." She got up and went to the counter.

After about ten minutes she returned with a white ceramic cup barely larger than a thimble. But there was nothing small about the aroma. She rested cup and saucer on the tabletop. "What now?"

"Drink it, but be sure to leave the grounds in your cup."

"Ugh."

"You have to drink it," I told her. "We're going to be reading the grounds for you."

"So, I'm bonding with the coffee?"

"Something like that." I stifled a giggle at the look of revulsion that crossed her face as she sipped. "As you're doing that, think about what you want to ask the grounds."

"That's easy enough," she said. "Where am I headed with my classes and my career?"

"Have you drunk most of it now?"

She coughed. "I hope so."

I reached down into my backpack and pulled out a large paper clip. "This cup has no handle, and traditionally the handle is the point of orientation that represents the person getting the reading."

"And your paper clip will serve as a handle?"

"No, but it can represent you." I looked into the cup and determined that there was just enough liquid left for a good reading. "Take the cup, turn it upside down, and place it on the saucer."

"That slop will get all over the table."

"Never mind. Just do it."

She did as I said, with only a small mess on the saucer and table.

"Okay?"

"Perfect. Now lift the cup and turn it upright again." After she did this, I said, "Take the paperclip and mark that place on the cup closest to you at this moment."

"This is what's supposed to be the handle," she said. "It's me, really."

I nodded. "Now let's see what the grounds have to tell us."

I looked into the cup to make a preliminary reading. "Amazing," I said. "You really do have the world in your cup."

Her eyes widened. "What do you mean?"

I moved my chair closer to her, pointing out the symbols I saw with a plastic coffee stirrer. "What we see towards the rim are events in the near future or the present. The further down in the cup a symbol appears, the farther away in time it is from you. Those symbols which are closest to the handle..."

"...paper clip..."

"...represent influences that are strongest on you. Make sense?"

"Actually, yes, given an initial acceptance that this reading is for real."

"You also need to consider whether a symbol is to the left of the…uh…paper clip, or if it is to the right. Images on the left are past and images on the right are what is becoming."

She was quiet for a moment. "I think I get it."

Taking the stirrer, I pointed to the grounds in the left side of the cup. "I see a gun and a bull as significant factors," I told her, outlining the symbols with the stirrer. "This strongly suggests past discord with friends and family."

"That's true enough," she said in surprise. "My whole adolescence was like that."

"However, I also see a candle. This represents a light in the darkness. Perhaps this is the drive you have within that has brought you to this point?"

"Well, nobody else brought me here."

"But here in the middle, and very close to the paper clip, I can see a bear, a foot, and a face. This suggests strength, change, and an ability to walk away from the past."

"Would that be connected to the candle?"

"Do you think it is?"

"Seems logical."

"Then let the connection stand. Here is the really interesting part, the things in your future."

"This is where I get skeptical." She paused. "Although it's been reasonable so far."

"Well, it's a good forecast," I said. "Clearly we have a bell and an acorn."

"I can see them!"

"Good, because they suggest future prosperity and healing."

She sat back, cupping her chin in her hand, mulling over the experience. "So is there an overall meaning to this, do you think?"

I nodded with conviction. "Your life was full of stress as far as your personal relationships, but you've lifted yourself out of that mess, and if you stay your course, you will be rewarded."

Staying silent, she kept working it out in her mind. Laughing, she leaned forward. "Well, I'm not an absolute convert," she told me, "but there's definitely a logic to this I never could see before."

"So I'm not crazy?" Grinning, I raised my eyebrows.

"Well," she said, looking me in my eyes, "I'm not sure I would go that far."

Skinny tall latte, double short no-cap mocha without, cappuccino with nutmeg, café au lait, double espresso, no matter how we order, we all know that we are talking about *coffee,* the drink that keeps us powered up and active.

Until this point, we have been concentrating on *tea leaf* reading. Tea is the second most popular drink in the world, just after water, and coffee comes in third. In Armenia, Greece, Turkey and many areas in the Arab world, tasseomancy using coffee grounds is practiced, and you can try this as well.

One of our resource people, Hakim from Aman, Jordan, told us his aunt would read fortunes at the end of family meals. Coffee was served in small cups after dessert. Every coffee cup always had a thick layer of grounds at the bottom. On a signal from the aunt, everyone would turn the mostly-empty cups over onto the saucers, spin the saucer three times, then turn the cup back upright. The aunt would then look into each cup and say something about what would happen in the coming week. Even though fortune telling is forbidden in Islam, the practice remains popular among regular people.

Coffee plant

The coffee plant is a shrub that grows up to thirty feet tall in the wild, but is kept to a height of about ten feet in cultivation. Coffee shrubs are originally from Ethiopia. Legend has it that sometime before 1000 BCE, a goatherd noticed one day that his animals were behaving strangely after eating the fruit and leaves of a certain large bush. The goats seemed full of energy and were running around excitedly. The goatherd also tried the leaves of the bush and he soon felt the same rush of energy and good spirits.

Intrigued by his discovery, the goatherd took some leaves and cherry-sized fruits to the abbot of a nearby monastery. Upon hearing the goatherd's story, the abbot put the leaves and fruits in some water and boiled them up. The resulting brew was so bitter that the abbot threw the contents of the pot onto the fire. When the fruits began to burn, they gave off a pleasant aroma—what we know today as the wonderful smell of freshly-brewed coffee. The abbot then had the idea of making a brew from the roasted fruit, and coffee as a drink entered the world.

Coffee beans: roasted and bean-cherries on a branch (inset).

Around 1000 BCE, Arab traders brought back coffee seeds to their homeland from the Ethiopian districts of Kaffa and Buno. They began to cultivate the plants on a large scale. The Arabs used the fruits, now called beans, to create the drink they called *qahwa*. The roasted beans themselves were called *bunn*, Arabic for "brown, coffee-colored." The main center of *qahwah* production was the city of Mocha in Yemen.

The secret of the invigorating brew was strictly guarded by the Arabs. Nevertheless, coffee plants were smuggled out of Arabia into other countries, even as far away as India where descendants of early plants were recently discovered near Mysore. Today we can find coffee plants from the Caribbean to Indonesia.

In 1453, the Ottoman Turks introduced coffee to Constantinople. The first coffee shop in the world, Kiva Han, opened in 1475. The Turks often added spices such as clove, cinnamon, cardamom and anise to their coffee. They also liked to grind the freshly-roasted beans to the consistency of very fine sawdust.

Around 1600, Italian merchants introduced caffè into the West, and in 1645, the first coffeehouse opened in Italy. By 1652, a coffeehouse had opened in London, and by 1672, in Paris. Coffee reached the New World in the 1660s and replaced beer as the favorite breakfast drink in New York by 1668.

Qahwa: coffee in Arabic

The various names for coffee all derive from the Arabic *qahwa*: French *café*, Dutch *koffie*, Finnish *kahvi*, Polish *kawa* /ka:-va/, Japanese *koohii*, Malay *kopi*, Thai *gafae*, and so on.

When it came time to name the coffee plant scientifically, Linnaeus simply Latinized the name to *Coffea*. The species was named *arabica*; people thought at the time that the shrub came originally from Arabia. The Web site of the International Coffee Organization, http://www.ico.org/, has a wide range of information about the history and botany of coffee.

If you enjoy a hot cup of Turkish coffee, strong and sweet with considerable "mud" on the bottom, then you know what the grounds look like when you have drained your cup. Coffee grounds tend to be smaller and finer than tea leaves, so care must be taken to allow them to settle completely before turning the cup over.

In order to practice tasseomancy on the grounds remaining at the bottom of a cup, it is essential that there be grounds. Modern coffee makers with their efficient filters were conceived to prevent the grounds from pouring out with the liquid. We solve this in one of two ways.

The first way is to brew coffee in the Turkish manner. *Turkish coffee* refers to the style of making coffee, rather than to any specific kind of coffee bean. We bring water to a boil on the stove, then add the coffee. We find that about one tablespoon of coffee for every six ounces of water is a good ratio. Freshly ground coffee is best to use, but feel free to experiment. Obviously, instant coffee is not a good choice since it does not have true grounds and the solid material will dissolve completely in the water.

Once you have added the coffee to the water, bring it back to the boil. This is an important step: if you do not boil the grounds, they will remain floating on top of the water. The longer you boil the coffee, the stronger it will be, so your own preference will be a guide here. At this point, Turks often add sugar and perhaps ground cardamom. You could even add milk or cream since the grounds will remain quite visible at the bottom of the empty cup.

The second way to be sure you have something to read in the cup is to scoop a teaspoonful of coffee grounds from the filter of your automatic coffee maker and stir them into a few ounces of coffee remaining in the cup of the person whose reading you are doing. The grounds will settle quickly and the person can sip the rest of the coffee, being careful to stop while there is still enough liquid to wet the grounds.

For both methods, you can stir the coffee as much as you want. The grounds will quickly settle on the bottom of the cup again. Some readers prefer to have the client stir the grounds personally, believing that this personal connection to the grounds will allow for a better reading.

For coffee-ground reading, an old-fashioned coffee cup is best, the kind that is shallow and wide. A light-colored china cup is best; darker cups will obscure the distribution of the grounds. Coffee mugs are often too deep for a good reading. In a mug it is difficult to see how the grounds are arranged, and the steep sides will keep the grounds trapped in the bottom.

When doing a reading, a certain amount of ceremony is appropriate. Once the cup has been drained, the person whose reading is being done will turn the cup upside down on the saucer. Some readers ask their clients to turn the cup and saucer three times counterclockwise turning the cup rightside up again. They then tell their clients to close their eyes, cover the cup with their hands and, without speaking aloud, either make a wish or ask a question. Then both the reader and the client will look into the cup.

You will see that the grounds have arranged themselves in what appear to be random patterns. In some ways, interpreting the grounds will seem to be like a caffeine-based Rorschach test, in which the same shapes can be understood differently by various observers. Two tasseomancers reading the same cup may have interpretations that vary widely, but may both be true in some sense.

The actual reading is similar to interpreting tea leaves, and the shapes will have the same meanings. Coffee-ground readers often say that interpreting coffee grounds is more like looking at clouds in the sky and finding shapes in them. Traditionally, the closer to the bottom of the cup the shape is, the farther away in time it will occur. Shapes at or above the middle of the cup are closer to us in time.

For the most part, coffee grounds are held to speak about the future. Occasionally, the grounds will seem to relate to something in the client's past. It is generally best for the reader to explain what he or she sees without limiting the reading in time. It is important to remember that, as the reader, you do not have to account for every last grain of coffee grounds in the bottom of the cup. Frequently, there is a lot of "static" in the cup, grounds that are not essential to the reading.

It is also essential to remember that reading coffee grounds in a cup is a pleasant way to end a meal or to spend some time with friends. Readings should not become overly serious or negative. The experienced reader knows what to say and what to pass over in silence. If, as you inspect the grounds in a cup, you feel compelled to announce that a major medical problem is looming, you should perhaps couch it as a suggestion to pay a visit to a physician.

As with reading tea leaves, certain shapes have accepted meanings. In Chapter Eight we set out a list of shapes and meanings for tea leaves, and these shapes retain the same significance when they appear in coffee grounds. Below is a short list of some frequently-appearing shapes and their interpretations:

Arch	– success in business, money arriving
Box, Container	– you have attracted someone
Bread	– work for your dreams, desires, hopes
Bridge	– need to make a decision
Circles, Coins	– money is coming to you
Diamonds	– marriage, material wealth
Flowers	– happiness
Fruit	– creativity, fertility, abundance
Harp	– romance

Heart	– a love affair (*A split/misshapen heart means unhappiness.*)
Knots	– problems, concerns, health worries
Road	– opportunities, moving on to new adventures
Ship	– a business opportunity

Top, left to right: heart, ship; *bottom, left to right:* diamond, two coins.

When you sit across from someone and gaze into that person's coffee cup, you will sense that there is more to tasseomancy than a mechanical recitation of shape and equivalent meaning. The activity creates a bond between two people, and you must be open to the feelings you receive from the other person. In some ways, searching the ground for shapes allows you to relax your mind and become more receptive to the thoughts and emotions of the person across from you. When you begin to speak, your words will come as much from your sensitivity to the other person as from what you see in the grounds.

We have chosen to talk about coffee-ground tasseomancy, but various cultures use other beverages. Among the Maya, divination using the residue from hot chocolate was used to reveal details of the past, present and future in a simple cup. Given the creative nature of human beings, probably any substance that leaves something behind in an emptied cup will suggest meaning.

Tea Time!
hands-on adventures

1. Okay, it's time to give coffee a try! Brew some coffee, let the grounds settle in a bit of remaining coffee at the bottom of the cup, invert the cup, put it back on the saucer, and do a reading.

2. Did you find reading coffee grounds different from reading tea leaves? Were the symbols clear? What differences did you note?

3. Since you are obviously an adventurous person—you've read the book this far — why not try to do a reading with another beverage? You just need to find something that leaves a residue in the cup, such as hot chocolate. Keep track of the similarities and differences.

4. Did you find that the tea leaf symbols were applicable to the other beverages as well? Were you able to add some new symbols and shapes to your notebook?

5. Why do you think tea leaf reading is far and away the most popular form of tasseomancy? Is there something special about brewing tea that helps add to the ambience? Would you ever prefer to use coffee grounds?

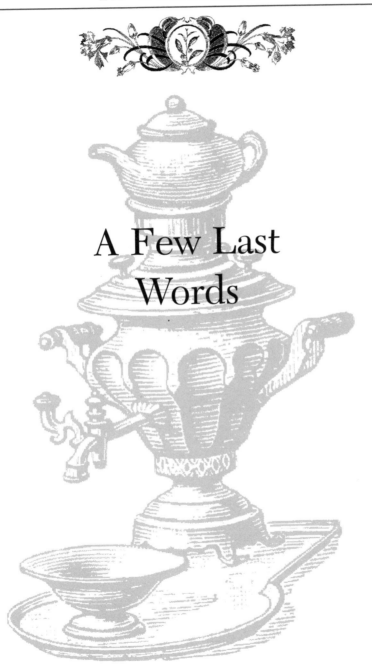

A Few Last Words

Although no form of divination should be practiced in haste, tasseomancy requires an especially careful preparation and great dedication on the part of the reader. This extra effort is not without commensurate reward. Tasseomancy will not only reveal the unseen world to you, but it will allow you to explore the depths of your own psyche and come to understand yourself better.

It has been our experience that those who practice tasseomancy gain a fuller respect for the variability of future events and tend to season their readings with caveats on the uncertainties of divination. We have also come to realize that the reader in tasseomancy brings a good deal to the table. The reader's mindset, feelings and concentration all guide the interpretation of the symbols in the cup.

To read tea leaves is to expand your mind. In these times when a lack of vision prevails, the art of tasseomancy is a perfect discipline for the open and seeking mind.

Where To Find It

A s we did the research for this book, we came upon a large number of Internet sites containing all sorts of information. Below we have listed our favorites.

TEA

- Coffee Bean Direct   http://www.CoffeeBeanDirect.com
(Don't let the name throw you off. We use Coffee Bean Direct for our own tea supplies.)

- Bigelow   http://www.bigelowtea.com

- Twinings   http://www.twinings.com/en_int/index.asp

- Peets Coffee & Tea   http://www.peets.com
(Stores in: Northern and Southern California, Oregon, Illinois, Massachusetts, Washington, Colorado)

- Lipton   http://www.lipton.com

EQUIPMENT

- Simpson and Vail   http://www.svttea.com
(Teapots, tea strainers, etc.)

- Cook's Corner   http://www.cookscorner.net
(Infusors, tea, etc.)

- Fantes   http://fantes.com/
(This is a world-famous kitchen supply store in and around Philadelphia, PA, with great selection of teapots and other tea equipment. This is the homepage; scroll down the list on the left until you reach "tea.")

- Harney and Sons   http://www.harney.com
(Has a wonderful tasting room)

BEYOND TEAPOTS AND SUCH

We also found that tea isn't just for drinking anymore! The art of serving and enjoying tea is perhaps more popular than it has ever been. For every kind of person, there seems to be a kind of tea and a way to savor it- black tea, green tea, herbal tea, medicinal tea, oolong, white, fruit, rooibos. You can get in on the fun of the tea renaissance by visiting the following websites.

- Victorian Trading Company
http://www.victoriantradingco.com/
(While Victorian does not specialize in tea, it does feature various teas as well as serving ware and other suggestions for a classic Victorian tea.)

- The Tea Man's Tea Talk
http://www.teatalk.com
(This colorful site is brought to you by true tea lovers. The site offers a lot of information on tea in a friendly manner.)

- The Tea Home Page
http://www.tea.co.uk
(Coming from the United Kingdom, this site specializes in tea education, health, and industry.)

- Stash Tea Company
http://www.stashtea.com
(In addition to selling tea and serving equipment, this site also provides plenty of information on all aspects of tea.)

- TeaMuse
http://www.teamuse.com
(Welcome to your gateway into the increasingly popular world of talking tea online. There is a monthly newsletter, information on using tea in cooking, a chat network, and a directory of tea rooms.)

- Upton Tea Imports

  http://www.uptontea.com
  (Importing a wide variety of loose teas and accessories.)

- Dilmah Tea

  http://www.dilmahtea.com
  (This is a family enterprise in Sri Lanka that exports the best tea around the world.)

- TeaInfo

  http://www.teainfo.org
  (The world of tea is broken down, discussed, and explained in this informative website.)

- Yogi Tea

  http://www.yogitea.com
  (This site offers exotic teas, green tea, chai tea, and the wonderful herbal teas for which Yogi Tea is famous among herbal healers.)

Books

We did a lot of fact-checking and reading as we wrote this book. Just in case you might like to read further, here are a few books we found informative about tea.

• *The Tea Companion: A Connoisseur's Guide*, Jane Pettigrew, Running Press Book Publishers (September 30, 2004)

• *The Book of Tea*, Kakuzo Okakura, Dover Publications (June 1, 1964)

• *The Book of Afternoon Tea*, Lesley Mackley, HP Trade (July 31, 1992)

❋ ❋ ❋